Hedda Schulz

From CA
to CAS ONLINE

© VCH Verlagsgesellschaft mbH, D-6940 Weinheim (Federal Republic of Germany), 1988

Distribution:

VCH Verlagsgesellschaft, P.O.Box 1260/1280, D-6940 Weinheim (Federal Republic of Germany)

Switzerland: VCH Verlags-AG, P.O.Box, CH-4020 Basel (Switzerland)

Great Britain and Ireland: VCH Publishers (UK) Ltd., 8 Wellington Court, Wellington Street,
Cambridge CB1 1HW (Great Britain)

USA and Canada: VCH Publishers, Suite 909, 220 East 23rd Street, New York,NY 10010-4606 (USA)

ISBN 3-527-26866-9 (VCH Verlagsgesellschaft)   ISBN 0-89573-815-5 (VCH Publishers)

Hedda Schulz

From CA
to CAS ONLINE

With a Contribution
by H.R. Pichler

Dr. Hedda Schulz
Handschuhsheimer Landstraße 64
D-6900 Heidelberg

Production Manager: Dipl.-Ing. (FH) Hans Jörg Maier

Library of Congress Card No. 86-24676

British Library Cataloguing in Publication Data

Schulz, Hedda.
From CA to CAS ONLINE.
1.Chemistry. Information retrieval services.
Chemical abstracts. Use
I. Title II. Von CA bis CAS ONLINE. English
025'.0654
ISBN 3-527-26866-9
ISBN 0-89573-815-5 U.S.

CIP-Kurztitelaufnahme der Deutschen Bibliothek

Schulz Hedda:
From CA to CAS online / Hedda Schulz. – Weinheim ; Basel
(Switzerland) ; Cambridge ; New York, NY : VCH, 188
  Dt. Ausg. u.d.T.: Schulz, Hedda: Von CA bis CAS online
  ISBN 3-527-26866-9 (Weinheim) Pp.
  ISBN 0-89573-815-5 (New York) Pp.

Druck: betz-druck gmbh, D-6100 Darmstadt
Bindung: Josef Spinner, Großbuchbinderei GmbH, D-7583 Ottersweier
Printed in the Federal Republic of Germany

Preface to the English Edition

The English edition is a translation of the book "Von CA bis CAS ONLINE". In addition, it contains a comprehensive chapter which provides numerous practical examples outlining the use and command language of CAS ONLINE. This chapter is. an extract from H.R. Pichler's book: "Online-Recherchen für Chemiker"; it has been updated and revised.
The remaining chapters of this book, including the sample searches, have also been updated and revised. Even if some examples do not contain the lastest information they are still valid, as this area of the CAS system has not been changed.
I wish to tank Mrs. Elizabeth Mole for the care she has taken in translating this book and preparing the proofs for printing. Her contribution to this book has been invaluable.

Heidelberg, October 1987   Hedda Schulz

Translator's Note

Being British, I have translated this book using British spelling. I am aware that the spelling in the descriptive text is sometimes inconsistent with that used in the figures and citations, most of which are taken from the literature (or databases) of the Chemical Abstracts Service. It is important, especially for the CAS ONLINE searcher, to note the discrepancies between the British and American spelling, as failure to do so could lead to an incomplete search, e.g. when the system does not recognize a search term because of spelling differences.

Preface

With the advent of online access to chemical databases a dream seems to have come true for the scientist in the field of chemistry: he only has to draw a chemical structure on a computer screen and press a key to ascertain whether a substance has been documented and what, when, and where information is available about it. So the searcher is naturally very disappointed if he does not obtain all the available literature references at once; and he tends to be prejudiced against the database! If a computer search proves complicated, if the dream is far removed from reality, the searcher often resorts to a manual search in the library to ensure that everything important is found. In general, the scientist unconsciously adapts his search strategy when seeking printed information. He begins with a subject term, the name of a chemical substance or a fact and according to the amount of information he finds he broadens, narrows or changes his search terms. It is obvious that this procedure is unsuitable for a computer search. In the course of online searches the searcher proceeds from the original term, as through a tunnel, to the target information. If the information obtained is inadequate or too extensive, the search strategy must be deliberately modified. In many cases an effective strategy is only then worked out. As this process is not consciously and systematically learned from searching through printed literature, it is difficult for the scientist to develop adequate search strategies for retrieving electronically stored information. The result is that online searches cost unnecessary time and money, or that dissatisfaction eventually leads the searcher to abandon his computer search.

This book shows that these difficulties are relatively easily overcome. Only two conditions must be fulfilled:

1. The searcher must be able to evolve a systematic search strategy. If he is a chemist he can quickly and easily learn how to do this from the volume indexes and other Chemical Abstracts Service publications. Those who have not learned to carry out a systematic search in printed literature will not be able to make effective and exhaustive use of online services; in particular those of the Chemical Abstracts Service.

2. The searcher must be familiar with the scope, the organization and the inner structure of the database before he begins his search. After all, no one would expect to find apples on a pear tree, but this is just the kind of mistake that is repeatedly made in computer-assisted searches.

The first part of the book explains the organization of Chemical Abstracts and illustrates how to obtain "hidden", abbreviated items of information. The development of search strategies is presented, with examples from many areas of chemistry, together with appropriate excerpts from Chemical Abstracts. In the second part the reader learns all the important facts about computer-readable files and online access to Chemical Abstracts Services and about the suppliers of these services. Examples of searches in CAS ONLINE illustrate the difference between searches in the printed literature and in online services. Those who plan a computer-assisted search should have read the second part of the book before they decide on which database to use. The database supplier then provides information tailored for the database being offered but, for the reader without a solid background knowledge, the introductory books from the supplier are often difficult to understand and the instructions hard to carry out.

This book is intended for students of chemistry and all those who have to solve their literature problems in chemistry and related fields.

I would like to thank Prof. Dr. D. Rehm for his numerous suggestions and especially for his help in the preparation of the examples for online searches. I am grateful to Mrs. Marion Schulz for her patient and conscientious preparation of the printing proofs.

Heidelberg, February 1985   Hedda Schulz

Contents

1 The Information System of the Chemical Abstracts Service

1.1 The History of Chemical Abstracts

The first reference journal in the field of chemistry was published in Germany: under the editorship of Gustav Theodor Fechner the "Pharmaceutisches Centralblatt" was first issued in 1830. It was renamed the "Chemisch-Pharmaceutisches Centralblatt" in 1850, a title more appropriate to its subject matter. From 1856 onwards the German Chemical Society published the "Chemisches Zentralblatt" which continued until 1969. In 1907 the American Chemical Society appointed a staff member of the National Bureau of Standards to make the results of research throughout the world accessible to chemists and those interested in chemistry in the USA. It was a necessary step because by far the most publications appeared in the German rather than the English language. This led to the foundation of the nonprofit organization known as the Chemical Abstracts Service (CAS). That same year the first issue of the Chemical Abstracts (CA) appeared. It contained 12,000 Abstracts about scientific publications, almost 50 % of which originated in Germany.

A scientific report in the field of chemistry or chemical engineering appears somewhere in the world today every minute, that is 500,000 publications annually. More than 60 % of these publications are in English, 15.7 % in Russian, 4 % in Japanese; 3.4 % are written in the German language.

The increase in the amount of chemical literature since Chemical Abstracts was first issued is illustrated in Fig. 1, which shows the number of abstracts published annually.

What began as a national organization with the aim of providing all chemically relevant information to American chemists has become an international service. Apart from CAS there is no organization, and thus no other reference journal outside the Soviet Union, which documents almost all the publications in the field of chemistry (approximately 98 % of the chemically relevant information worldwide). There is hardly a comparable institution which provides such systematic and thorough coverage of knowledge in other scientific fields. Today the Chemical Abstracts Service employs about 1,200 people, more than a third of whom are chemists.

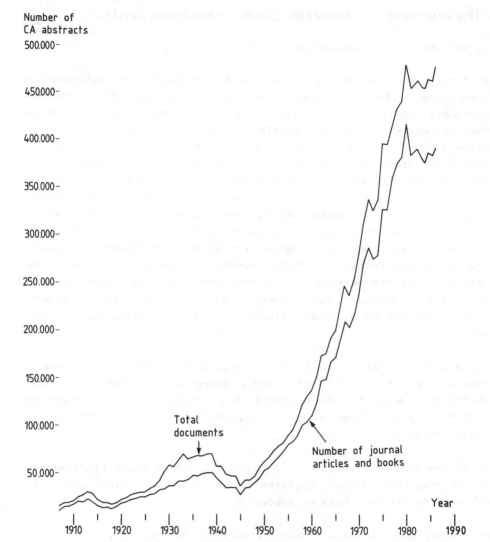

Fig. 1: Number of scientific papers included in Chemical Abstracts
        from 1907 to 1986

1.2 How an Abstract in Chemical Abstracts is Created

The information for the Chemical Abstracts Service is obtained from
approximately 12,000 journals from more than 140 countries as well as
patent documents, conference proceedings, research reports and books
from all over the world. The source of these abstracts is not always
the field of chemistry, many come from physics, mathematics, technol-

ogy, the geosciences and life sciences. However, only those publications directly related to chemistry or chemical engineering are taken
into account. The "document analyst" who often has to understand very
uncommon languages, records a summarized version of the publication
and the appropriate entries for the various indexes on audio-tape.
These texts and information, together with the bibliographic data, are
stored on computer-readable magnetic tapes by means of special computer terminals and later – after any necessary corrections – they are
transferred to computer storage. Each abstract is read by at least
three different chemists, and various computer programs automatically
check for spelling mistakes in the recorded text. A sign inserted
after the appropriate word indicates that the term is as yet unknown
to the system i.e. that it is a possible spelling error. Abbreviations
are also automatically inserted. When the text of the abstract has
been thoroughly checked, the computer arranges it into the proper
format for publication, justifies and hyphenates the text, makes-up
pages, sorts the index entries alphabetically and composes the material on film from which offset printing plates are produced.

Approximately three months after publication of a research paper the
corresponding abstract appears. Articles due to appear in the most important international chemical journals are processed considerably
faster so that the abstract sometimes appears before the journal itself is published.

1.3 The Databases of the Chemical Abstracts Service

As early as the 1960s the Chemical Abstracts Service began to develop
a highly automated processing and production system for the information collected. As a result it became possible to provide a variety of
information services related to specialized fields. Thus the world's
first computer-produced periodical, Chemical Titles, was introduced in
1961.

The bibliographic CA database has been compiled since 1967. It includes all the index entries from Chemical Abstracts, complete bibliographic information, and text of all the abstracts published since
1970 as well as the texts of one million abstracts which appeared
between 1967 and 1970. This database is now accessible for online
searches (cf. 7.3, p. 141).

Since 1965 all chemical substances mentioned in the literature have been recorded according to the CAS Registry System. A CAS Registry Number is assigned to each new substance which, however, provides no information about the chemical structure of the substance (e.g. the number for water is 7732-18-5). The CAS Registry Number has a characteristic organization: up to 6 digits precede the first hyphen, between the two hyphens there are two digits, after the second hyphen there is a check number (cf. 4.1, p. 108).

The two-dimensional structural formula, stereochemical descriptors, all labelled atoms and unusual valences are recorded for each substance, i.e. for each Registry Number. In addition, the molecular formula, the CA Index Name used in the indexes of Chemical Abstracts, and all trivial and trade names known to the Chemical Abstracts Service are linked to the CAS Registry Number. Today this database comprises more than 8.4 million chemical substances, of which 75 % are mentioned only once in the literature, and more than 12 million substance names. Seventeen substances each have more than 150 names and one substance, polyethylene, has more than 1,500. Of the documented substances 88 % are unequivocally defined, 2 % only partly defined (in general, these are substances in which the position of substituents, double bonds or ester groups is not exactly known) and 3 % are only recorded by name or molecular formula, as their structure has either not yet been fully resolved or the resolution has not yet been published (these are mostly natural substances). 4 % of the substances are polymers, 2 % are alloys, and less than 1 % are mixtures. 75 % of the approximately 8 million substances contain at least one ring in their structural formula, 24 % are substances exhibiting stereochemistry.

By means of this CAS Registry File it is possible to ascertain whether or not a substance with a certain name has already been mentioned under another name. In the course of registration for Chemical Abstracts about 6,000 substances are checked daily. If not yet registered, the structural formula of the new substance is first stored. The substance is then awarded a systematic CA Index Name based on IUPAC[1] rules, and the rules of the Chemical Abstracts Service, by a nomenclature expert (cf. 2.1.3, p. 25). About 520,000 new substances

---

IUPAC[1]: International Union of Pure and Applied Chemistry

are registered each year. Like the CA File, this CAS Registry File is accessible for online searches (cf. 7.3, p. 141).

Since the 1970s the Chemical Abstracts Service has compiled information about developments in management, marketing, and production in the chemical and allied industries. Furthermore, laws and rules applying to this industrial field have been extracted from the appropriate industry and economics journals and recorded in the database of chemical economics literature.

The comprehensive CAS information system has been developed from all the databases of the Chemical Abstracts Service (Fig. 2). In the following chapters the contents of the numerous information services of the Chemical Abstracts Service will be discussed in detail and, in particular, their use will be demonstrated with the aid of several examples. The success of a literature search - whether manual or computer-assisted - depends on how exactly and, at the same time, flexibly the searcher can state his problem. This means that he must not only find the precise terminology for the chemical fact or substance being sought, but also determine all possible aspects under which the subject of his search could be mentioned or researched. These two considerations must not necessarily be resolved prior to the search for literature. In fact, they constitute the first step in the search itself and can be carried out with the aid of Chemical Abstracts or, more precisely, with the indexes to Chemical Abstracts. However, this necessitates a thorough knowledge of the particular indexes and the searcher must be aware of which information - even in abbreviated form - is contained in which index.

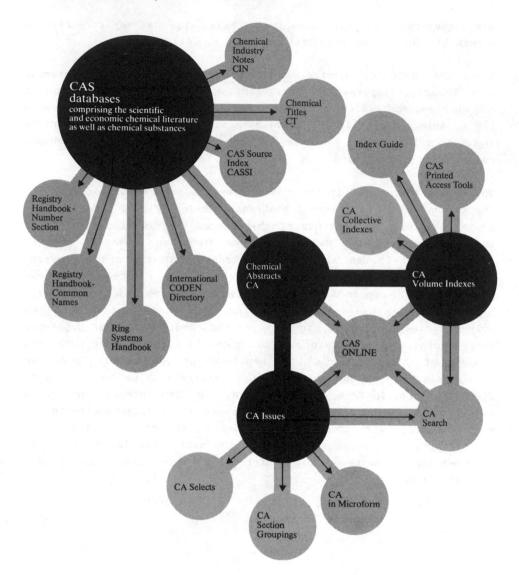

Fig. 2: The CAS information system

2 Searching for Literature in Chemical Abstracts

2.1 Organization of Chemical Abstracts

Today, Chemical Abstracts (CA) is the world's best-known and most comprehensive reference periodical for all areas of chemistry and chemical engineering. It consists of two parts: the abstracts and the indexes.

2.1.1 CA Issues

The Abstracts

Each publication containing new information of importance to chemistry or chemical engineering is abstracted in Chemical Abstracts. The individual abstracts are divided into two parts: the first part comprises all the important bibliographic particulars, the second the abstract text. The latter is organized as follows: the first sentence summarizes the new research results reported in the publication. The rest of the abstract highlights the following information:
- purpose and scope of the reported work
- new reactions, substances, techniques, procedures, apparatus, and properties
- new applications
- results of the investigation together with the author's interpretations and conclusions.
The terminology, e.g. the substance names, employed in the abstract is taken over from the original document and does not necessarily correspond to the systematic nomenclature of the Chemical Abstracts Service.

The Chemical Abstracts Service divides the original publications into seven different categories:
1. Journal articles
2. Congress and symposia proceedings and edited collections of their papers
3. Technical reports
4. Deposited documents
5. Dissertations
6. New books and audio-visual material
7. Patents

The various types of abstracts differ especially in their bibliographic data (Figs. 3 to 10).

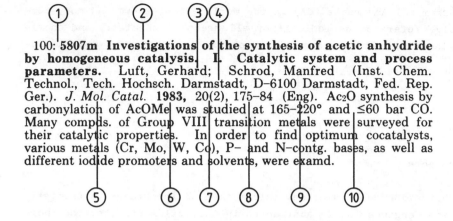

Fig. 3: Abstract of a journal article

    1.   CA volume and abstract number
    2.   Document title
    3.   Authors' names
    4.   Address of the location where the reported work was done
    5.   Journal title
    6.   Year of publication
    7.   Volume and, if applicable, issue number of the journal
    8.   Inclusive pagination of the article
    9.   Language of the original document
   10.   Abstract text

Some journal articles are reviews which are not abstracted, but the number of cited references is shown (Fig. 4).

100: **7071r New natural amino acids.** Wagner, Ingrid; Musso, Hans (Inst. Org. Chem., Univ. Karlsruhe, D-7500 Karlsruhe, Fed. Rep. Ger.). *Angew. Chem.* **1983,** 95(11), 827-39 (Ger). A review with 104 refs.

Fig. 4: Citation of a review article

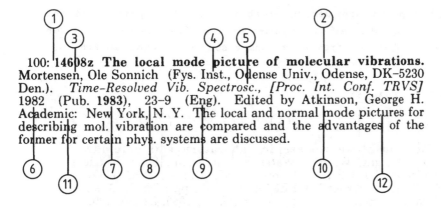

Fig. 5: Abstract of proceedings and edited collections of their
papers

    1. CA volume and abstract number
    2. Document title
    3. Author's name
    4. Address of the location where the reported work was done
    5. Title of the proceedings book or collection
    6. Date of the meeting
    7. Date of publication
    8. Inclusive pagination of the publication
    9. Language of the original document
  10. Editor's name
  11. Publisher's name, city and state or country of publication
  12. Abstract text

Names and complete addresses of publishers who are frequently named in
Chemical Abstracts are listed under the heading of "Directory of Publishers and Sales Agencies" in the CAS Source Index.

Technical reports are generally abstracted from primary literature sources. In exceptional cases, however the Chemical Abstracts Service extracts the abstract from a secondary source as shown in Fig. 6.

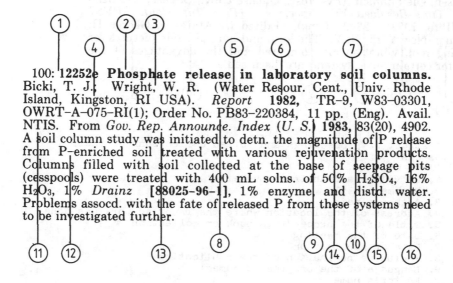

100: 12252e **Phosphate release in laboratory soil columns.** Bicki, T. J.; Wright, W. R. (Water Resour. Cent., Univ. Rhode Island, Kingston, RI USA). *Report* **1982**, TR-9, W83-03301, OWRT-A-075-RI(1); Order No. PB83-220384, 11 pp. (Eng). Avail. NTIS. From *Gov. Rep. Announce. Index* (*U. S.*) **1983**, 83(20), 4902. A soil column study was initiated to detn. the magnitude of P release from P-enriched soil treated with various rejuvenation products. Columns filled with soil collected at the base of seepage pits (cesspools) were treated with 400 mL solns. of 50% H_2SO_4, 16% H_2O_3, 1% *Drainz* [88025-96-1], 1% enzyme, and distd. water. Problems assocd. with the fate of released P from these systems need to be investigated further.

Fig. 6: Abstract of a technical report
  1. CA volume and abstract number
  2. Document title
  3. Authors' names
  4. Address of the location where the reported work was done
  5. Identification of document as a technical report or tech-
     nical report series title
  6. Date of publication
  7. Report number
  8. Order number
  9. Inclusive pagination of the report
 10. Language of the original document
 11. Source of the original document
 12. Abstract text
 In the case of abstracts from secondary sources:
 13. Title of the secondary document
 14. Date of publication of the secondary document
 15. Volume and issue number of the secondary document
 16. Abstract number of the secondary document

The source from which a document can be obtained is identified by an Availability Code. A list of Availability Codes is to be found in the introduction to the first issue of a CA volume. When no code is given for technical reports, deposited documents or dissertations, then the title itself has been included in the CAS Source Index and the appropriate sources for ordering the document are shown there.

Deposited documents can be published in one of two ways:

1. The document is cited in the primary literature in the form of a title announcement only, i.e. without abstract, synopsis, or summary.

2. The document is announced in the secondary literature, e.g. in a catalogue of deposited documents.

The abstract and the index entries are prepared from the complete paper.

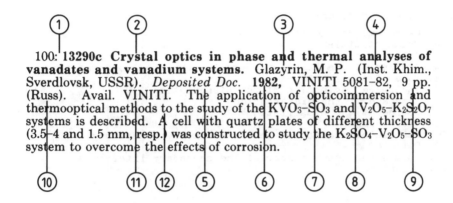

Fig. 7: Abstract of deposited documents

     1. CA volume and abstract number
     2. Document title
     3. Author's name
     4. Address of the location where the reported work was done
     5. Identification of document as a deposited document
     6. Date of publication
     7. Specific document citation
     8 Number of the deposited document
     9. Inclusive pagination of the document
    10. Language of the document
    11. Availability Code
    12. Abstract text

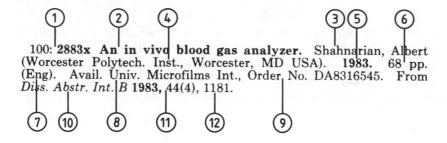

① ② ④   ③⑤   ⑥

100: 2883x **An in vivo blood gas analyzer.** Shahnarian, Albert (Worcester Polytech. Inst., Worcester, MD USA). **1983.** 68 pp. (Eng). Avail. Univ. Microfilms Int., Order No. DA8316545. From *Diss. Abstr. Int. B* **1983,** 44(4), 1181.

⑦ ⑩   ⑧   ⑪   ⑫   ⑨

Fig. 8: Heading of a dissertation
     1. CA volume and abstract number
     2. Document title
     3. Author's name
     4. Address of the location where the reported work was done
     5. Date of publication
     6. Inclusive pagination of the dissertation
     7. Language of the dissertation
     8. Source of the dissertation
     9. Order number
In the case of a citation in the secondary literature:
     10. Title of the secondary document
     11. Volume and issue number of the secondary literature
     12. Pagination

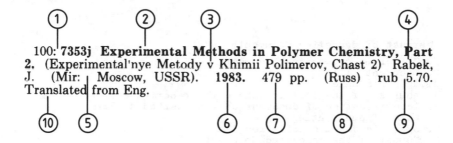

① ② ③ ④

100: 7353j **Experimental Methods in Polymer Chemistry, Part 2.** (Experimental'nye Metody v Khimii Polimerov, Chast 2) Rabek, J. (Mir: Moscow, USSR). **1983.** 479 pp. (Russ) rub 5.70. Translated from Eng.

⑩ ⑤   ⑥ ⑦ ⑧ ⑨

Fig. 9: Announcement of new books and audio-visual material
     1. CA volume and abstract number
     2. Title of the book (always in English)
     3. Title of the book in the original language
     4. Name of the author or editor
     5. Name and address of the publisher
     6. Year of publication
     7. Number of pages in the book
     8. Language of the book
     9. Original price
     10. If the book is a translation, the language from which it
         has been translated is shown

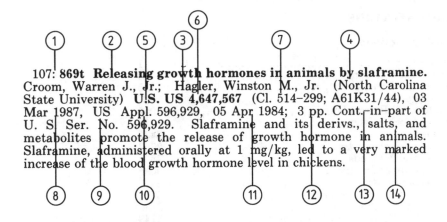

Fig. 10: Abstract of patents

    1. CA volume and abstract number
    2. Patent title (in CA it is often an augmented or reworded
       version of the original title)
    3. Names of the inventors
    4. Name of the assignees
    5. Country in which the patent was granted
    6. Patent number
    7. Patent classification - for U.S. patents, both the U.S and
       the International Patent Classification (IPC) symbols are
       given
    8. Date of patent publication
    9. ISO country code for the country of priority
    10. Patent application number
    11. Date of patent application and, if applicable, foreign
        and/or domestic priority numbers
    12. Number of pages
    13. Reference patent or application number of another legally
        related domestic document, the relationship is indicated
        by addition, division, continuation, reissue, etc
    14. Abstract text

A Chemical Abstracts issue is published every week. However, the entire field of chemistry and chemical engineering is covered by two
consecutive issues, i.e. the subject matter is repeated every fortnight.

ABSTRACT SECTIONS

Biochemistry Sections

Organic Chemistry Sections

Fig. 11: CA Sections in each odd-numbered issue

ABSTRACT SECTIONS

Macromolecular Chemistry Sections

35.	Chemistry of Synthetic High Polymers	7168
36.	Physical Properties of Synthetic High Polymers	7448
37.	Plastics Manufacture and Processing	7579
38.	Plastics Fabrication and Uses	7913
39.	Synthetic Elastomers and Natural Rubber	8140
40.	Textiles	8285
41.	Dyes, Organic Pigments, Fluorescent Brighteners, and Photographic Sensitizers	8473
42.	Coatings, Inks, and Related Products	8522
43.	Cellulose, Lignin, Paper, and Other Wood Products	8750
44.	Industrial Carbohydrates	8893
45.	Industrial Organic Chemicals, Leather, Fats, and Waxes	8911
46.	Surface-Active Agents and Detergents	8969

Applied Chemistry and Chemical Engineering Sections

47.	Apparatus and Plant Equipment	9019
48.	Unit Operations and Processes	9121
49.	Industrial Inorganic Chemicals	9383
50.	Propellants and Explosives	9473
51.	Fossil Fuels, Derivatives, and Related Products	9534
52.	Electrochemical, Radiational, and Thermal Energy Technology	9905
53.	Mineralogical and Geological Chemistry	10098
54.	Extractive Metallurgy	10397
55.	Ferrous Metals and Alloys	10536
56.	Nonferrous Metals and Alloys	10993
57.	Ceramics	11440
58.	Cement, Concrete, and Related Building Materials	11715
59.	Air Pollution and Industrial Hygiene	11850
60.	Waste Treatment and Disposal	12045
61.	Water	12181
62.	Essential Oils and Cosmetics	12415
63.	Pharmaceuticals	12468
64.	Pharmaceutical Analysis	12719

Physical, Inorganic, and Analytical Chemistry Sections

65.	General Physical Chemistry	12766
66.	Surface Chemistry and Colloids	12966
67.	Catalysis, Reaction Kinetics, and Inorganic Reaction Mechanisms	13141
68.	Phase Equilibriums, Chemical Equilibriums, and Solutions	13280
69.	Thermodynamics, Thermochemistry, and Thermal Properties	13385
70.	Nuclear Phenomena	13436
71.	Nuclear Technology	13831
72.	Electrochemistry	14340
73.	Optical, Electron, and Mass Spectroscopy and Other Related Properties	14554
74.	Radiation Chemistry, Photochemistry, and Photographic and Other Reprographic Processes	15188
75.	Crystallography and Liquid Crystals	15424
76.	Electric Phenomena	15787
77.	Magnetic Phenomena	16397
78.	Inorganic Chemicals and Reactions	16613
79.	Inorganic Analytical Chemistry	16771
80.	Organic Analytical Chemistry	16935

Fig. 12: CA Sections in each even-numbered issue

SECTION 60

WASTE TREATMENT AND DISPOSAL

A. Coverage in this Section includes:

1. Chemistry, composition, treatment, and disposal of industrial wastes and
   sludges. (See C.1)

> "Industrial wastes" are defined here as those materials
> produced during or left over from a manufacturing process or
> industrial operation. The material is not usable for the
> ordinary or main purpose of manufacture.

2. Chemistry, composition, treatment, and disposal of municipal wastes and sludges.

3. Chemistry, composition, treatment, and disposal of laboratory wastes.

4. Chemistry, composition, treatment, and disposal of domestic wastes
   (e.g. treatment systems for homes, motor homes, and boats).

5. Design and operation of incinerators.

B. Alternative Placing and Specific Exclusions

1. Studies dealing with those so-called wastes from which specific
   materials are recovered should be placed in the section which ordinarily
   deals with those materials (e.g., recovery of hydrochloric acid and iron
   oxide from pickle liquor: Section 49 (Industrial Inorganic Chemicals)).

2. Radioactive wastes: Section 71 (Nuclear Technology).

C. Cross-References

1. A.1 - Cross-reference appropriate section covering the corresponding
   industrial process.

D. Subsection Arrangement

0. Reviews

1. Biological treatment processes

2. Chemical treatment processes

3. Physical treatment processes

4. Treatment of nonaqueous materials

5. Disposal of untreated and treated wastes

6. Other

Fig. 13: Definition of CA Section 60 (excerpt from the Subject
        Coverage Manual)

The Chemical Abstracts Service categorizes the whole field of chemistry and chemical engineering into 5 Section Groupings and a total of
80 Subject Sections: Sections 1 to 34 are included in CA issues with
odd numbers (Fig. 11), Sections 35 to 80 in each even-numbered issue
(Fig. 12).

The scope of the individual Sections is precisely defined. In the
"Subject Coverage and Arrangement of Abstracts by Sections in Chemical
Abstracts", or "Subject Coverage Manual" for short, each Section is
described in detail (Fig. 13):
- the coverage of a Section is described under A
- areas which, by definition, are excluded from this CA Section are
  listed in B
- the possibilities of cross-referring to other Sections are to be
  found under C
- D shows how the content of the abstract or, to be more precise, of
  the original paper determines the sequence of abstracts within the
  Section. This information about subsections can be used for online
  searches.

The arrangement of the abstracts within any one section in Chemical
Abstracts is determined by the original document type (first, abstracts of journal articles, including citation of review articles,
then abstracts about technical reports, deposited documents and dissertations, followed by announcements of new books and, finally, patent abstracts). The abstracts under the various document headings are
arranged according to the content of the original publication (Subsections).

Each Section ends with a list of cross-references to other Sections
and abstracts of related interest. The cross-references are arranged
in the order of Section numbers, but subdivided to indicate whether
they are patent or other abstracts.

The CA Issue Indexes

Each Chemical Abstracts issue contains three indexes:
- Keyword Index
- Patent Index
- Author Index.

All these indexes, but particularly the Keyword Index, differ from the half-yearly volume indexes. The entries in the issue indexes are extracted from the abstract text, not from the original literature. Thus, these indexes do not provide such in-depth and systematic coverage as the volume indexes.

The **Keyword** Index consists of a series of words and phrases selected from the title and text of the abstract (Fig. 14). Subject terms and substance names are listed alphabetically. The substance names included in the Keyword Index seldom correspond to the systematic CA Index Names. They can be trivial or semi-systematic names, but are, in each case, the designations used by the author in his paper and thus also included in the CA abstract. Only the volume indexes of the Chemical Abstracts contain the systematic substance names.

The issue indexes are indispensable in the search for the most up-to-date literature, as it is not always possible to wait for the publication of the volume indexes. It is, however, advisable to repeat the search with the aid of the volume index, as the systematics of the volume indexes offer greater reliability.

The **Patent Index** is arranged in an alphabetic list of the abbreviated names of the countries in which the patents were issued. Within the listing for each country the patent numbers are arranged in numerical order. The principle of the Patent Index, which was introduced in 1981 to replace the Numerical Patent Index and the Patent Concordance, is to document the complete history of the patent family relating to each patent. The degree of interrelationship is indicated by the addition of phrases like: "related", "non-priority" or "continuation-in-part".

KEYWORD INDEX   *Vol. 100, No. 2, 1984*

Bergamot
   oil cosmetic P 12443t
Bergapten
   essential oil P 12443t
   sunscreen phototoxicity 12435s
Berkelium
   248 level calcn 13570u
   3 sepn purifn extn 16843w
Bertholet
   reaction phenol detn spectrophotometry
      16972n
Beryllium
   aluminum master alloy 11037b
   alumocreson chromoxane blue P 16735n
   americium source coincident neutron
      14182f

Fig. 14: Excerpt from the Keyword Index of a Chemical Abstracts issue

The Chemical Abstracts Service covers all patents dealing with aspects of chemistry or chemical engineering from 29 patent offices in 19 countries[1] around the world and two international institutions[2] into account. Patents of relevance to chemistry and chemical engineering from a further eight countries[3] are abstracted only if the patent applicant is resident in these countries.

---

[1] Australia
   Austria
   Belgium
   Brazil
   Canada
   France
   German Democratic Republic
   Germany, Federal Republic of
   India
   Israel
   Japan
   Netherlands
   People's Republic of China
   Rumania
   South Africa
   Switzerland
   Union of Soviet Socialist Republics
   United Kingdom
   United States of America

[2] European Patent Organization
   World Intellectual Property
   Organization

[3] Czechoslovakia
   Denmark
   Finland
   Hungary
   Norway
   Poland
   Spain
   Sweden

Fig. 15 shows an excerpt from the Patent Index of a Chemical Abstract issue. The only difference from entries in the volume index is that some items are printed in boldface type. This either indicates a completely new patent which is abstracted in the same issue, or refers to the extension of a patent family or to a change in status of a patent application. The use of boldface type draws attention to the latest information supplied to the Chemical Abstracts Service that week.

PATENT INDEX   Vol. 100, No. 2, 1984

DE (Germany, Federal Republic of)

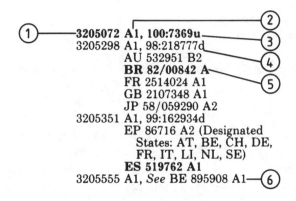

Fig. 15: Excerpt from the Patent Index of a Chemical Abstracts issue

    1. Patent number
    2. Document Code: this indicates what stage has been reached in the application process for that particular patent e.g. whether it is an unexamined patent or a patent application. Explanations about the application status are contained in the first issue of each Chemical Abstracts volume and in the introdution to the Patent Index of a CA volume.The document code is individually explained for each country as its meaning can differ.
    3. Abstract number: this line in boldface type means that this is a new patent, the abstract of which appears in the same CA issue.
    4. Listing of a patent family, of which the German patent was the first to be sent to the Chemical Abstracts Service and thus first abstracted.
    5. A new member of the patent family: this entry within the patent family in boldface type indicates that this Brazilian patent, which is related to the German patent, has just been presented for examination.
    6. Cross-reference to a patent family to which the German patent belongs. The first patent in the family to be abstracted was a Belgian patent which appeared in an earlier Chemical Abstracts issue. This entry indicates that the application of the German patent was sent to the Chemical Abstracts Service during the preparation period of that particular Chemical Abstracts issue.

The **Author Index** in a Chemical Abstracts issue (Fig. 16) lists the surnames of the authors in alphabetical order, followed by their initials, and the names of patent applicants. Patent abstracts are characterized by the letter P preceding the abstract number.

AUTHOR INDEX   *Vol. 100, No. 1, 1984*

Hochstein P 149p 325t 1139x
Hochwald G M 4315n
Hockwin O 4007p
Hocmanova M 1414h
Hodes R J 4401n
Hodgen G D 897f
Hodgson J R 1911t
Hodgson K O 2720s
Hoebeke J 4541h
Hoechst A.-G.   P 5284p
      P 6057d   P 6079n   P 6081g
      P 6201w   P 6503w   P 6542h

Fig. 16: Excerpt from the Author Index of a Chemical Abstracts issue

In the first issue of each CA volume the abstracts part is explained, each index is preceded by a description of its organization. Every fortnight, i.e. in each odd-numbered issue, there is a list of the journals and other publications which have been covered by Chemical Abstracts for the first time or which have changed their title or mode of publication. This information is compiled and subsequently appears in the supplements to the CAS Source Index (cf. 3.1, p. 100).

2.1.2 Index Guide

The most important tool to aid the user of Chemical Abstracts is the Index Guide (Fig. 17). It is the indispensable key to the volume indexes and should be consulted before beginning any literature search.

The Index Guide is a work of reference providing cross-references to the various CA volume indexes. It is not itself an index as it does not refer directly to abstract numbers. It comprises an alphabetically ordered collection of subject terms, synonyms, acronyms, trivial and trade names, all concepts which are not used in the strictly controlled vocabulary of the indexes. For instance, an entry may refer to the corresponding systematic substance name as used in the CA volume indexes, or give a cross-reference to the subject term used in the General Subject Index. Moreover, since the 1986 edition, the Index Guide contains all terms from the controlled vocabulary without any additional information, so that the user can tell at a glance whether or not a term belongs to the controlled vocabulary. Furthermore, the Index Guide describes indexing rules which can provide practical guidelines for literature searches. It also helps the user to find the appropriate heading under which a subject or substance is recorded in the volume or collective indexes of Chemical Abstracts.

1982–1986 INDEX GUIDE

Atomic weight and mass
Studies of atomic weight and mass themselves, or of
the atomic weights and masses of classes of
elements, are indexed at this heading. For
atomic weights and masses of specific
elements, see headings for those elements
of nuclides——see *Atomic nuclei*, mass of
Atomiron 44MR
See *Iron [7439-89-6]*, powd.
Atomite
See *Carbonic acid calcium salt (1:1) [471-34-1]*
Atomization
The spraying process is indexed at this heading.
Decomposition of compounds to atoms is
indexed at such headings as *Dissociation,
Photolysis, Thermal decomposition.*
Sputtering processes are indexed at
Sputtering
enthalpy of——see *Heat of atomization*
Atomizers
Atom-probe microanalysis
See
Mass spectroscopy
field-ionization, microprobe

Fig. 17: Excerpt from the Index Guide

The basic rules and practices which apply to Chemical Abstracts and the indexes are described in the Appendices to the Index Guide:
Appendix I: Hierarchies of General Subject Headings (arranged
                     both according to subject areas, and alphabetical-
                     ly)

Appendix II: Organization and Use of the indexes to Chemical Ab-
                    stracts
Appendix III: Selection of General Subject Headings
Appendix IV: Chemical Substance Index Names (rules for the se-
                    lection of systematic CA Index Names)

The Index Guide appears at the beginning, and a cumulative one at the
end, of each collective period of Chemical Abstracts (the twelfth collective period covers 1987 to 1991). Every eighteen months a cumulative edition of the Index Guide is published which replaces the previous one.

2.1.3 CA Volume Indexes

Two volumes of Chemical Abstracts each containing 26 issues are pub-
lished annually. Thus, comprehensive volume indexes are issued twice a
year containing the following individual indexes:
- General Subject Index
- Chemical Substance Index
- Formula Index
- Index of Ring Systems
- Author Index
- Patent Index

Up until 1972 only one Subject Index appeared. It contained substances
as well as subject terms. In order to facilitate the search for literature, this extensive index was subdivided. Today the Subject Index is
issued in three parts: the General Subject Index, the Chemical Substance Index and the Index Guide. Information about literature published before 1972 is all included in the Subject Index.

As the success of a literature search depends on the effective use of
the various volume indexes, it is essential to be familiar with all
the details of the information as it appears in the volume indexes.

General Subject Index

The General Subject Index contains no specific substance names (these belong in the Chemical Substance Index), but refers to more general subjects like:
- classes of chemical substances
- subject terms
- physical and chemical phenomena
- reactions
- chemical technology
- industrial processes and equipment
- scientific designations for animals, plants, micro-organisms and
- biological and medical terminology.

The General Subject Index (Fig. 18) differs considerably from the Keyword Index (Fig. 14) in the CA issues.

At first glance two groups of information can be differentiated:
1. the index headings (in boldface print)
2. the index entries, or text modifications (in lightface print).
The vocabulary of the index headings is subject to rigid control, in contrast to that of the index entries. These text modifications to the individual abstracts are extracted from the original paper and thus contain the nomenclature and terminology of that particular author. They are phrases from natural language. Before beginning a literature search about a general subject it is necessary to ascertain whether the concept sought belongs to the controlled vocabulary and can therefore be found as an index heading in the General Subject Index. The Index Guide is indispensable for this purpose.

The General Subject Index frequently contains concepts expressed in broad, general terms. Consequently, these concepts are followed by a long list of abstract citations. In order to help narrow a search, such index headings are allocated heading subdivisions. For instance, in the General Subject Index to Chemical Abstracts Vol. 92 there are forty pages of abstract citations under the heading of "blood". To avoid scanning through forty pages of index entries it is important to assign the search term to one of the subdivisions - the qualifiers. There are seven standard qualifiers:
- Analysis
- Biological studies
- Occurrence
- Preparations
- Properties
- Reactions

- Uses and miscellaneous

For special fields other appropriate subdivisions can be chosen - for biological and medical concepts the "Organ and Tissue" qualifiers are employed:
- Composition
- Disease or disorder
- Metabolism
- Neoplasm
- Toxic chemical or physical damage.

There are only two Radiation Qualifiers:
- biological effects
- chemical and physical effects

Fifteen categories appear at subdivided compound and compound-class headings (cf. p. 32).

For alloys only two categories are employed:
- base
- non-base.

These qualifiers and categories can occur in both the General Subject Index and the Chemical Substance Index.

A heading is sometimes directly followed by information indicating which abstracts are dealt with in the subsequent list and which are excluded. For example, after the heading "coordination compounds" only papers relating to coordination compounds as a class of substances are taken into account; documents about specific coordination compounds are not cited. These must be sought under the substance name, which means with the aid of the Chemical Substance Index.

After the index heading, and possibly a short explanation of its scope, announcements of new books are listed, each abstract number being preceded by the letter B. Abstract numbers beginning with R refer to reviews and the letter P identifies patent abstracts.

VOL. 98, 1983 – GENERAL SUBJECT INDEX

Boophilus microplus
> Southern cattle tick is also indexed at this
> heading
chitin of cuticle of, 31666z
control of
> on cattle, by Cyhalothrin, 121315p
> by flumethrin, 12895g
> by flumethrin–contg. spray formulation, P
> 156420w
ethion resistance and control of, in New Caledonia,
> 211526n
neuron activity of, acaricides effect on measurement
> of, 48524z
resistance to pyrethroids in, mechanism of, 193345w
Boops boops
potassium transport by erythrocyte of, A23187 and
> calcium effect on, 50803h
Borago officinalis
biol. active compds. of, high–altitude adaptation in
> relation to, 122867g
rosmarinic acid of, 141942u
Borates
> Studies of borate salts as a class are indexed at
> this heading. For subclasses (e.g., alkali metal
> borates), specific salts, and esters, see the acid
> headings, such as *Boric acid* (HBO_2)
227106m
adsorption of, from water, nickel hydroxide for,
> 204114y
anhyd., crystal structure, 19631b

Fig. 18: Excerpt from the General Subject Index

Chemical Substance Index

The largest discrepancy in terminology between CA abstracts, the CA
issue index and the appropriate volume index occurs in the substance
names. The Chemical Substance Index employs only the systematic CA
Index Names for substances, not the trivial or semi-systematic names
generally used by an author in his paper. The Chemical Abstracts
Service assigns systematic CA Index Names to each substance mentioned
in Chemical Abstracts and to all additional substances from the original literature not mentioned in Chemical Abstracts. These names are
based on the nomenclature rules of IUPAC. However, IUPAC rules are
frequently out of touch with the latest chemical knowledge so that the
Chemical Abstracts Service must establish its own rules and usage in
accordance with the IUPAC nomenclature system. Thus a searcher must
ensure that he knows the systematic Index Name of a substance or how
to find it before he begins his search.

Once again the Index Guide is indispensable for this purpose, and in this case in two ways: either the user finds the trivial or trade names in the alphabetic section of cross-references with the appropriate reference to the CA Index Name, or he attempts - and this is much more difficult - to derive the systematic Index Name based on the nomenclature rules in Appendix IV himself. These rules of nomenclature also appear as a separate small publication for each collective period under the title "Naming and Indexing of Chemical Substances for Chemical Abstracts". The most marked changes in the systematic CAS nomenclature were made at the start of the ninth collective period, i.e. at the beginning of 1972. Thus, completely different CA Index Names may be encountered when searching for literature which appeared before 1972.

The fundamental principles of CAS nomenclature and the systematic CA Index Names will be briefly explained using two examples. Index Names are primarily arranged under the heading of the functional parent compound, followed by the substituents in alphabetical order, the name modification to the parent compound and, finally, the stereochemical descriptor, when necessary. The parent compound, characterized by its functional group, of the substance

$$NH_2-CH_2-CH-CH-CH_2-SO_3-CH_2-CH_3$$
$$\underset{\displaystyle Cl}{|} \quad \underset{\displaystyle NH_2}{|}$$

is 1-butanesulfonic acid. (An appropriate reference to the name of the parent compound is given in the alphabetic section of the Index Guide, Fig. 19). A comma after the parent compound indicates the inversion of the name. The two substituents are called "amino" and "chloro". In the alphabetic arrangement of the substituents the prefix indicating the number of the substituents (e.g. di-) is not taken into account. Thus the substituents are designated "2,4-diamino-3-chloro" in this case. Thereafter follows the modification: "ethylester".

The systematic name of the above mentioned substance is:
     2,4-diamino-3-chloro-1-butanesulfonic acid, ethylester.
The inverted systematic CA Index Name is:
     1-butanesulfonic acid, 2,4-diamino-3-chloro-, ethylester.

1982 INDEX GUIDE

Sulfonic acids
  Studies of sulfonic acids as a class are indexed at
    this heading. For studies of specific sulfonic
    acids, see those specific headings. Individual
    sulfonic acids are named by appending the
    suffixes –sulfonic acid, –disulfonic acid, etc., to
    the name of a parent compound such as an
    acyclic hydrocarbon, ring system or ring
    assembly, e.g., *Methanesulfonic acid,*
    1,3–Benzenedisulfonic acid, [1,1'–Bipheny⊃
    l]–4,4'–disulfonic acid. The following classes
    of acids (cited in descending order) are ranked
    higher than sulfonic acids: peroxy, carboxylic,
    carbothioic, carbohydrazonic, and carboximidic
    (see note at *Carboxylic acids*). When any such
    acid is present in the molecule, the sulfonic
    acid moiety is expressed as a sulfo radical, e.g.,
    Benzenecarboximidic acid, 4–sulfo–;
    1–Naphthalenepropanoic acid,
    5–(sulfomethyl)–. Alkanesulfonic acids
    attached directly to ring systems by single
    bonds are indexed at conjunctive names such
    as *Benzeneethanesulfonic acid,* or as described
    in more detail by the note at *Methanesulfonic*
    acid
  See also
      Carboxylic acids
        sulfonated
      Oils
        sulfonated
  ligno——see *Lignosulfonic acid [8062-15-5]*
Sulfonic acids, uses and miscellaneous
  surfactants
    see such headings as
      Detergents
      Flotation agents
      Foaming agents

Fig. 19: Excerpt from the Index Guide

The inversion of names is one of the basic principles in forming the
CA Index Names, as the Chemical Substance Index is arranged alphabetically according to parent compounds. This greatly facilitates the
search for similar substances since they must all be shown under the
same parent compound heading. It is therefore especially important to
recognize the parent compound, e.g. whether the following substance is
a diamine or a derivative of an acid:

The name of the parent compound is always chosen to correspond to the highest ranking functional group.

The classes of compounds are arranged in the following hierarchical sequence (in descending order):

1. Free radicals
2. Cationic compounds
3. Neutral coordination compounds, including metallocenes
4. Anionic compounds
5. Acids in the order of the central atom given by the sequence:
   C, S, Se, Te, O, P, As, Sb, Si, B
6. Acid halides etc. initially arranged in the order of acids (cf. 5), and then for each individual acid: fluoride, chloride, bromide, iodide, azide, isocyanate, isothiocyanate, isocyanide, cyanide
7. Amides, in the order of the above-mentioned acids (cf. 5)
8. Nitriles, in the order of the above-mentioned acids (cf. 5)
9. Aldehydes
10. Ketones
11. Alcohols and phenols
12. Hydroperoxides
13. Amines
14. Imines
15. Compounds of N, P, As, Sb, Bi, B, Si, Ge, Sn, Pb, O, S, Se, C

Thus, the structural formula illustrated above shows a derivative of an acid, a nitrile. As the longest continuous chain or cyclic structure also belongs to the parent compound, it is called: 4-morpholinepropanenitrile with the substituent α-[(dimethylamino)-methyl] -. Fig. 20 shows the appropriate excerpt from the Chemical Substance Index.

If the substance in question is regarded as a nitrile of propionic acid the systematic CA Index Name for it is: propanenitrile, 3-(diethylamino)-2-(4-morpholinylmethyl)-. The compound is not to be found in the Chemical Substance Index under this name (Fig. 21).

1972–1976 CHEM. SUBSTANCE INDEX

4-Morpholinepropanenitrile [*4542–47–6*]
  83: 206186n
  antiozonants, for rubbers, **85:** P 64468w
  catalysts, for polyurethane foam manuf., **82:** P
    99084h

   •
   •
   •

——, α-[(**3,4-dimethoxyphenyl)methylene**]–
    [*30077–72–6*], **79:** P 42545t; **83:** P 78855r
——, α-[(**dimethylamino)methyl**]– [*35961–71–8*], **76:**
    99594a
  compd. with 2,4,6-trinitrophenol (1:2) [*36546–62–0*],
    76: 99594a
——, $\alpha,\alpha,\beta,\beta$-**2,2,3,3,5,5,6,6-dodecafluoro**–
    [*51579–53–4*]
  condensation of, with ammonia, **81:** P 105583t
  cyclocondensation with ammonia, triazine deriv. by,
    80: 95897m
——, β-**methyl**– [*38405–81–1*], **77:** 139984g
  compd. with 2,4,6-trinitrophenol (1:1) [*38405–83–3*],
    77: 139984g

Fig. 20: Excerpt from the Chemical Substance Index

However, under certain circumstances it may be sensible to name a
parent compound contrary to IUPAC rules. This is the case when a
structural unit other than the parent compound defined according to
the IUPAC system is of interest. The inversion of systematic Index
Names in the Chemical Substance Index is extremely useful in the
search for derivatives or compounds related to certain substances. It
depends entirely on the searcher's decision as to which substituent
and which parent compound is important. This is the only way to search
for substructures in the printed version of Chemical Abstracts. In
general, however, it is advisable to select the parent compound heading with the highest ranking functional group, as the higher the functional group the more substitutions and derivatives are listed under
it.

The systematic subdivision found in the Chemical Substance Index is
analogous to that of the General Subject Index: the substance names
printed in boldface type are subject to the rules of nomenclature,
i.e. they are the CA Index Names, while the index entries in lightface
type originate from the natural language generally used by the author
in his publication, they are not part of the controlled vocabulary.

Propanenitrile,

——, **3-(diethylamino)–** [*5351–04–2*], **79:** 125727e
activity in, of hydrocarbons, extn. selectivity in
    relation to, **85:** 131351t

    •

    •

    •

——, **3-(diethylamino)–2-[(diethylamino)methyl]–**
    [*35961–65–0*], **76:** 99594a
compd. with 2,4,6–trinitrophenol (1:2) [*36404–08–7*],
    76: 99594a
——, **3-[2-(diethylamino)-1-[(diethylamino)=**
    methyl]ethoxy]–
dihydrochloride [*51734–33–9*], **80:** 107919k
——, **3-[2-(diethylamino)-1-[(dimethylamino)=**
    methyl]ethoxy]– [*51735–45–6*], **80:** 107919k
dihydrochloride [*51734–32–8*], **80:** 107919k
——, **3-[[2-(diethylamino)ethyl]amino]–**
    [*41832–86–4*]
reaction of
    with 5–carbethoxy–4–chloro–2–phenylpyrimidine,
        83: 178969z
    with 5–carboxyethyl–4–chloro–2–=
        phenylpyrimidine, **79:** P 32081z
    with chloropyrimidine, **82:** P 43455n
——, **2-(diethylamino)-2-methyl–** [*35672–46–9*], **78:**
    28744e; **79:** 91744r
Strecker synthesis of, kinetics of, **83:** 8666f
——, **2-[3-(diethylamino)-4-methyl-5-oxo-2-=**
    benzoxepin-1(5*H*)-ylidene]– [*40750–49–0*],
    78: 136020z
——, **3-(diethylamino)-2-nitro–** [*58132–73–3*]
prepn. and cyclization of, **84:** 59123e
——, **3,3'-[[4-[[[4-(diethylamino)phenyl]imino]=**
    methyl]phenyl]imino]bis– [*56133–58–5*], **83:** P
    50773p

Fig. 21: Excerpt from a Chemical Substance Index

Some substance names, under which a large number of abstracts are cited, are divided by heading subdivisions which are arranged according to two criteria:

1. the subject of the publication in which the particular substance is mentioned (qualifiers),

2. the functional group of the substance (categories).

The same standard qualifiers as in the General Subject Index are applied:
1. Analysis
2. Biological studies
3. Occurrence
4. Preparations
5. Properties
6. Reactions
7. Uses and miscellaneous

The subject-orientated qualifiers concerning a substance name, e.g. benzoic acid (Fig. 22), are succeeded by the following possible categories:

1. Acetals	– very limited use
2. Anhydrides	– for acid headings
3. Anhydrosulfides	– for thio acid headings
4. Compounds	– for addition compounds, complexes, mixtures, salts, solid solutions, reaction products and for a few unusual functional derivatives which cannot be assigned to any other category
5. Derivatives (general)	– for nonfunctional derivatives, which are not sufficiently identified for complete naming
6. Esters	– for acid and alcohol headings
7. Ethers	– used only for specific carbohydrate headings: cellulose, dextran, glycogen and starch
8. Hydrazides	– for acid headings
9. Hydrazones	– for aldehyde and ketone headings
10. Lactones	– for the stereoparents of hydroxy acids
11. Mercaptals	– for the stereoparents of aldehydes
12. Mercaptoles	– for the stereoparents of ketones
13. Oxides	– for amine headings
14. Oximes	– for aldehyde and ketone headings
15. Polymers	– for oligomers, homopolymers, and copolymers

If no qualifier or category is mentioned as a subdivision to a substance name it means that there is no abstract on this subject in that particular Chemical Abstracts volume.

VOL. 97, 1982 – CHEM. SUBSTANCE INDEX

Benzoic acid *[65–85–0]*, **analysis**
a.c. polarog. detection of, in reversed–phase ion–pair
high–performance liq. chromatog., 229491m
chromatog. of, cation–exchange liq., 20139h
cinnamoylcocaine sepn. from, by liq. chromatog.,
18521h

•
•
•

Benzoic acid *[65–85–0]*, **biological studies**
absorption of
by intestine, solvent drag effect in, 84703v
by intestine, solvent drag from water influx effect
on, 84652c
by intestine, water influx in relation to, 192726p
D–amino acid oxidase binding of
enzyme protonation in relation to, 140838g
FAD fluorescence response to, 195008s

•
•

Benzoic acid *[65–85–0]*, **occurrence**
biodegrdn. of, in lake water, sorption by clay
suspension in relation to, 168497u
mineralization of, in lake water and sewage,
133073a

Benzoic acid *[65–85–0]*, **preparation**
215938a
electrosynthesis of, from Ph halides, 39110p
formation of
by oxidn. of benzaldehyde, effect of catalysis on,
23054n
in oxidn. of o–xylene, 55072h

•
•

Benzoic acid *[65–85–0]*, **properties**
absorption and emission spectra of, in micellar
environments, 226251x
acidity and IR spectrum of, isokinetic relation
between, 38146t
adsorption of, on Silochrome modified with
polyoxyethylene and silanes, of arom. compds.,
98958u

•

Benzoic acid *[65–85–0]*, **reactions**
acid dissocn. of, in aq. methanol, liq. chromatog.
studies of, 29040b
N–acylation by, of leucylargininal di–Bu acetal, P
145287m

•
•

Benzoic acid *[65–85–0]*, **uses and miscellaneous**
antiwear aq. hydraulic fluid compn. contg., P
165889n

•
•

Benzoic acid, anhydrides
anhydride *[93–97–0]*
N–acylation by, of hydroxyisoxazolopyridine
deriv., P 182395r
addn. reaction of, with cyclic imidates, 127587e

•

**dianhydride with 1,4–butanediylbis[carbamic
acid]** *[83173–50–6]*, blowing agents, for plastic
foams, P 145781t
monoanhydride with phosphoric acid
[6659–26–3], reaction of, with
acylphosphatase, kinetics of, 68344y
Benzoic acid *[65–85–0]*, **compounds**
Specific coordination compounds containing the
benzoato ligand are indexed only at the
coordination headings, e.g., *Copper,
bis(benzoato–O)bis(isoquinoline)–*
[54775–57–4]. Nonspecific coordination
compounds containing this ligand are indexed
here and at the element headings. Specific
coordination compounds containing other
ligands derived from benzoic acid are indexed
here as well as at the specific coordination
headings
alkali and alk. earth metal salts, in pyridine–free
Karl Fischer reagent for water detn., P
155568t

•
•

thallium complex *[82446–98–8]*, P 92547n
zinc salt *[553–72–0]*
catalysts, for manuf. of cellular polyurethanes, P
199069k
stabilizers, contg. magnesium stearate, PVC
compns. contg., for packaging films, properties
of, 56622z
thermal recording paper color developer compns.
contg., P 31323q
zinc salt, mixt. with magnesium dioctadecanoate
[78615–63–1], stabilizers, PVC compns.
contg., for packaging films, properties of,
56622z
Benzoic acid *[65–85–0]*, **derivatives (general)**
alkyl derivs., in mutagenic wastewater treatment
plant effluents, 60412y
amino derivs., herbicides, patents for, 86938z
derivs.
detn. of, by potentiometric titrn. in pyrrolidone,
229496s

•
•

Benzoic acid *[65–85–0]*, **esters**
Simple esters (butyl, chlorophenyl, cyclohexyl,
decyl, 2–(diethylamino)ethyl,
2–(dimethylamino)ethyl, 1,1–dimethylethyl,
dodecyl, ethenyl, ethyl, 2–ethylbutyl,
2–ethylhexyl, heptyl, hexyl, methyl,
1–methylethyl, methylphenyl, 1–methylpropyl,
2–methylpropyl, nitrophenyl, nonyl, octadecyl,
octyl, pentyl, phenyl, 2–phenylethyl,
phenylmethyl, 2–propenyl, and propyl) are
indexed at this heading. Other esters are
indexed only at the alcohols
akyl esters, chromatog. of, on silylated silica
surfaces, 12405b

Fig. 22: Excerpt from a Chemical Substance Index

The CAS Registry Number is shown in square brackets after each substance name and each stereochemical descriptor. Thus the Chemical Substance Index is a rapid and inexpensive tool for ascertaining the CAS Registry Number of a particular substance in order to carry out an online search.

Formula Index

Guidelines for forming molecular formulae have also been established. The Chemical Abstracts Service writes its molecular formulae according to the Hill System which was published by Hill in 1900 (J. Amer. Chem. Soc. <u>22</u> (8), 1900, 478-494): for carbon-containing compounds, first the carbon atoms and then the hydrogen atoms are named, the remaining element symbols follow in alphabetic order. The element symbols of all other substances are arranged alphabetically. The Formula Index is arranged alphanumerically (Fig. 23).

VOL. 98, 1983 – FORMULA INDEX

C₃H₂NO
 2-Azetyloxy *[84648-84-0]*, 142735r
 3-Azetyloxy *[84648-83-9]*, 142735r
C₃H₂NO₂
 Acetic acid, cyano-
  ion(1-) *[23297-32-7]*, 16222h, 50963k, 96408m,
   178434f
C₃H₂NO₄
 Propanedial, nitro-
  ion(1-), sodium *[34461-00-2]*, 178508h, 215434d
C₃H₂N₂
 Propanedinitrile *[109-77-3]*. See *Chemical
  Substance Index*
C₃H₂N₂O
 Pyrazolone *[39455-90-8]*. For general derivs. see
  Chemical Substance Index
(C₃H₂N₂O)ₙ
 Poly(1,3,4-oxadiazole-2,5-diylmethylene)
  [83176-49-2], P 25573a

Fig. 23: Excerpt from a Formula Index

All substances mentioned in a particular Chemical Abstracts volume are listed in the Formula Index. Each molecular formula is followed by the various systematic CA Index Names, the appropriate CAS Registry Number in square brackets and the corresponding abstract numbers. Where numerous abstract citations are given for one substance name, so that subdivisions are necessary in the Chemical Substance Index, a cross-reference to the Chemical Substance Index is given.

The Hill System has been modified for several classes of substances (the following substances on the left are not mentioned in the Formula Index, they are to be found under the substance names on the right):

metal salts of acids $\longrightarrow$ free acids
metal salts of alcohols $\longrightarrow$ free alcohols
metal salts of organic bases $\longrightarrow$ free compounds
molecular addition compounds $\longrightarrow$ each individual component
                                                       (not under the total mole-
                                                       cular formula)
copolymers $\longrightarrow$ each monomer
mixtures $\longrightarrow$ individual components

In all these cases the substance is indexed under the name of the mo-ecular formula from which it was derived.

Though the Formula Index is one of the tools for determining the systematic substance names, it contains no text modifications to the individual abstracts. Thus the Chemical Substance Index should be consulted for further information once the systematic CA Index Name has been determined. When analogous compounds are sought, e.g. bro-mides and chlorides or ethyl and phenyl esters, the searcher should likewise turn to the Chemical Substance Index, as structurally related compounds are grouped together there.

The Formula Index and the Index of Ring Systems are both tools which enable the Chemical Substance Index to be used more effectively.

Index of Ring Systems

It is often particularly difficult to determine the systematic CA Index Names of cyclic compounds and find the desired compound in the Chemical Substance Index. In such cases the Index of Ring Systems can help. This index is restricted to the coverage of cyclic parent compounds; substituted compounds and very simple ring systems (e.g. ben-

zene and cyclohexane) are excluded. This means that cyclic parent
names are never accompanied by substituent prefixes of any kind, or by
functional suffixes in the Index of Ring Systems. Rings differing in
the position of hetero atoms, bridges, or fusion sides are listed
separately. Only one representative of a set of rings differing only
in the position of the indicated hydrogen is listed, i.e. only the
isomer with the indicated hydrogen in the lowest numbered, nonangular
position:

2H-Pyran   4H-Pyran   5H-Form   3aH-Form

5H-Furo [3,2-g] pyrazolo [1,5-c] [1,3]-
benzoxazine

The description of a ring system consists of three components (this is
called the ring analysis):
1. Number of component rings
    2. Ring size (number of atoms comprising a ring)
        3. Elemental analysis of the component rings (excluding
            hydrogen)
The ring analysis for the following compound is:

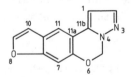

Number of component rings   4-Ring System
    Numbers of atoms per ring   5,5,6,6
        Atoms comprising the rings $C_3N_2-C_4O-C_4NO-C_6$
(The rings are arranged according to their size, even in the elemental
analysis. Rings of equal size are listed alphanumerically in the order
of their molecular formula according to the Hill System.)

It can be difficult to ascertain the number of rings in a large complicated ring system. There are two simple methods for determining
this number:

1. The number of bonds which must be broken to obtain an open chain system is equal to the number of rings.
2. The number of single bonds, minus the number of atoms in the ring system plus one equals the number of rings.   S−A+1 = N

Cyclic stereoparents comprising several ring skeletons are entered under the name of each cyclic skeleton which occurs in the substance (apart from the very simple ring systems like benzene and cyclohexane). For the substance salinomycin the ring analysis is:

3-Ring System   1-Ring System

   5,6,6   6

        $C_4O-C_5O-C_5O$ C_5O

Salinomycin is entered in the Index of Ring Systems under both ring analyses (Fig. 24).

VOL. 98, 1983 – IRS

1-RING SYSTEMS

6
  As₃P₃
    1,3,5,2,4,6-Triphosphatriarsenane
  As₆
    Hexarsenane
    •
    •
    •
C₅O
    Amphotericin B
    Decitol, 4,8-anhydro-
    Decitol, 6,10-anhydro-
    Dodecitol, 7,11-anhydro-
    •
    •
    •
⟶ Salinomycin
    Septamycin
    α-D-Tagatopyranose
    α-D-Talopyranose

3-RING SYSTEMS

5,6,6
  CN₂P₂-C₄P₂-C₆
    1,4-Methano-5*H*-2,3,1,4-benzodiazadiphosphe⸗
    pine
  CN₄-C₄N₂-C₆
    Tetrazolo[5,1-*a*]phthalazine
    Tetrazolo[1,5-*a*]quinazoline
    Tetrazolo[1,5-*c*]quinazoline
  C₂BO₂-C₆-C₆
    13,15-Dioxa-14-boradispiro[5.0.5.3]pentadecane
    •
    •
    •
  C₄O-C₅O-C₅O
    Furo[3,2-*b*]pyrano[2,3-*e*]pyran
    Spiro[furan-2(3*H*),2'(3'*H*)-pyrano[3,2-*b*]pyran]
    Acanthifolicin
    1,6,8-Trioxadispiro[4.1.5.3]pentadecane
    Noboritomycin A
⟶   Salinomycin
    5-Undeculo-5,9-pyranose, 2,6:8,11-dianhydro-

Fig. 24: Excerpt from the Index of Ring Systems

Thus, this CA volume contains abstracts about this substance or one or more of its derivatives. As no abstract numbers are given, the systematic CA Index Name obtained from the Index of Ring Systems is used to continue the search in the Chemical Substance Index which contains further information about the substance itself and possibly also about its derivatives.

Author Index

In the Author Index the names of all the authors whose publications are abstracted in that Chemical Abstracts volume are listed. Moreover, the names of patentees, industrial companies, societies, committees, government authorities, institutions and research organizations are also included. The Chemical Abstracts Service has established rules and conventions for the spelling and transliteration of authors' names. These conventions are explained in each Volume 1 of the Chemical Abstracts preceding the Author Index.

The Author Index accompanying a Chemical Abstracts volume is considerably more detailed than the Author Index in a CA issue (Fig. 25).

The author's surname together with his complete first name or names (if available) appears in boldface type. Surnames, but only the initials of the first names, are ordered alphabetically. A cross-reference, beginning with "see", often follows, indicating that the person was a coauthor and leading to the name of the primary author of that particular publication, as all titles and details of publications are given only under the name of the appropriate primary author. First the titles of the abstracted publications written by the author alone are listed in order of ascending abstract numbers. Thereafter follow the remaining publications arranged alphabetically according to the names of the coauthors. In the Author Index the complete titles of the publications are announced. The letters B and P preceding an abstract number denote that the source document is a book or a patent respectively.

VOL. 98, 1983 – AUTHOR INDEX

Armstrong, Donald James See Mok, Machteld C.
Armstrong, David Milton See Levey, Alan I.
——; Ross, C. A.; Pickel, V. M.; Joh, T. H.; Reis, D. J.
Distribution of dopamine–, noradrenaline–, and
adrenaline–containing cell bodies in the rat medulla
oblongata: demonstrated by the immunocytoch=
emical localization of catecholamine biosynthetic
enzymes, 65970j
Armstrong, David Thomas See Evans, Gareth;
Reddoch, R. B.; Walton, Elizabeth A.
——; Daniel, S. A. J.; Salhanick, A. R.; Rani, C. S. S.
Hormonal interactions in regulation of steroid
biosynthesis by the ovarian follicle, 11489r
——; Evans, G.
Factors influencing success of embryo transfer in
sheep and goats, 66200v
——; Pfitzner, A. P.; Warnes, G. M.; Ralph, M. M.;
Seamark, R. F.
Endocrine responses of goats after induction of
superovulation with PMSG and FSH, 191977e
Armstrong, Daniel Wayne See Boehm, Richard E.;
Sherma, Joseph
——; Bui, K. H.; Boehm, R. E.
Practice, mechanism and theory of reversed phase
TLC polymer fractionation, 108099b

Fig. 25: Excerpt from an Author Index

Patent Index

The Patent Index of a Chemical Abstracts volume results from the cumu-
lation of the individual issue indexes. However, the newly abstracted
patents are no longer printed in boldface type (Fig. 26).

VOL. 98, 1983 – PATENT INDEX

JP (Japan)

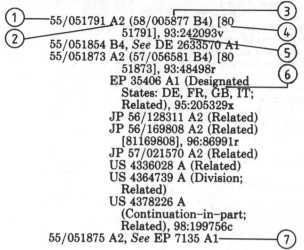

55/051791 A2 (58/005877 B4) [80
        51791], 93:242093v
55/051854 B4, *See* DE 2633570 A1
55/051873 A2 (57/056581 B4) [80
        51873], 93:48498r
    EP 35406 A1 (Designated
        States: DE, FR, GB, IT;
        Related), 95:205329x
    JP 56/128311 A2 (Related)
    JP 56/169808 A2 (Related)
        [81169808], 96:86991r
    JP 57/021570 A2 (Related)
    US 4336028 A (Related)
    US 4364739 A (Division;
        Related)
    US 4378226 A
        (Continuation–in–part;
        Related), 98:199756c
55/051875 A2, *See* EP 7135 A1

Fig. 26: Excerpt from a Patent Index
    1. Patent number
    2. Document Code, indicating which stage the application pro-
       cess has reached.
    3. The numbers in round brackets refer to an earlier stage
       in the application process. The patent was previously sub-
       mitted to the Chemical Abstracts Service under this number
       which was cited in the appropriate CA abstract. If the
       patent number has not changed in the course of the appli-
       cation process, only the previous Document Code is given
       in round brackets.
    4. The Gregorian calendar version of the Japanese patent num-
       ber is shown in square brackets. It is obtained by adding
       25 to the first two digits of the original Japanese number
       (to give the year according to the Gregorian calendar), as
       only patent numbers in the Gregorian calendar version are
       used in CA abstracts.
    5. CA volume and abstract number
    6. For a European patent the abbreviated names of the coun-
       tries to which the patent applies are shown. This European
       patent was itself abstracted. This means that the European
       patent includes several details or pieces of information
       which are not contained in the related Japanese patent.
       Only under such circumstances is a patent from a patent
       family abstracted a second or even a third time in Chemi-
       cal Abstracts.
    7. This Japanese patent belongs to a patent family of which
       the European patent was the first to be abstracted by the
       Chemical Abstracts Service. Further information about this
       patent family and the CA abstract number pertaining to it
       are to be found under the European patent number.

2.1.4 CA Collective Indexes

At the end of each five-year period - the last one ended in 1986 - the
ten CA volume indexes issued during that period are combined into a
single large collective index. It contains no additional information
(Fig. 27).

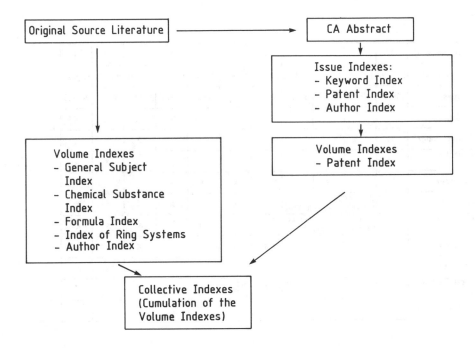

Fig. 27: Successive steps in the production of the CA indexes

Collective indexes are an invaluable tool in a retrospective literature search as they eliminate the repetition of identical steps which
would be necessary when using the appropriate volume indexes, and at
the same time they offer simultaneous access to several million abstracts. (The Tenth CA Collective Index with its 75 volumes was recorded as the largest index in the world by the Guinness Book of Records. It will be far surpassed by the Eleventh Collective Index with
a total of 93 volumes published in 1987.)

Like the volume indexes, the collective indexes are composed of various individual indexes. However, on account of scientific developments, the content and organization of the indexes have been considerably changed in the course of the 80-year history of the Chemical Abstracts Service (Fig. 28).

Collective Index	1.	2.	3.	4.	5.	6.	7.	8.	9.	10.	11.
Years covered	1907-16	1917-26	1927-36	1937-46	1947-56	1957-61	1962-66	1967-71	1972-76	1977-81	1982-86
CA Volumes	1-10	11-20	21-30	31-40	41-50	51-55	56-65	66-75	76-85	86-95	96-105
Index Guide								X	X	X	X
Gen. Subject Index									X	X	X
Chem. Substance Index									X	X	X
Subject Index	X	X	X	X	X	X	X	X			
Formula Index		27-Year Collective Formula Index (1920-1946)			X	X	X	X	X	X	X
Index of Ring System	(contained in the introduction to the Subject Index)						X	X	X	X	X
Author Index	X	X	X	X	X	X	X	X	X	X	X
Patent Index										X	X
Numerical Patent Index				10-Year Num. P. I.	X	X	X	X	X		
Patent Concordance							X	X	X		

Fig. 28: The Chemical Abstracts collective indexes

From the first to the seventh collective periods there was only one Subject Index, containing all the information available about subject terms and substances as well as cross-references to alternative substance names. Since 1967, the eighth collective period, the Index Guide has been issued. It provides cross-references and indicates relationships between the various substance names and subject terms. In 1972, the ninth collective period, the Subject Index was divided into the General Subject Index and the Chemical Substance Index. From that time onwards, it has been necessary to precisely determine whether a search should be subject- or substance-oriented.

During the 80 years' existence of Chemical Abstracts nomenclature has also undergone further development. A major revision of the CAS nomenclature system was undertaken at the beginning of the ninth collective period. If literature published before 1972 is sought, it is essential to determine the proper CA Index Name used at that time. The Index Guide is helpful for this purpose. Before its existence the appropriate information could be found in the Subject Index.

1982 INDEX GUIDE

Doryphornine
 See *1(2H)–Isoquinolinone, 7–hydroxy–6–*◦
  methoxy–2–methyl– [54302–47–5]
DOS
 See *Decanedioic acid, esters, bis(2–ethylhexyl)*
  ester [122–62–3]
Dosamix
 See *Urea, N'–(3–chloro–4–methoxyphenyl)–N,*◦
  N–dimethyl–, mixt. with 6–chloro–N,N'–◦
  diethyl–1,3,5–triazine–2,4–diamine
  [53126–75–3]

Fig. 29: Excerpt from the 1982 Index Guide

VOL. 98, 1983 – CHEM. SUBSTANCE INDEX

Decanedioic acid *(sebacic acid) [111–20–6]*
Decanedioic acid *[111–20–6]*, **analysis**
 detn. of
  in natural waters and wastewaters, by gas–liq.
   chromatog., 113387y
  in urine by gas chromatog., aciduria diagnosis in
   relation to, 85565j
Decanedioic acid *[111–20–6]*, **biological studies**
 of royal jelly, seasonal rhythm of, 104591h
 urinary calcium oxalate–contg. calculi dissoln. with, P
  83590q
 urinary oxalate and phosphate calculi formation
  inhibition by, urinary citrate excretion and
  urinary calcium binding capacity in relation
  to, 83384a
Decanedioic acid *[111–20–6]*, **preparation**
 manuf. of, with *Torulopsis candida*, P 124202k
•
•
•
Decanedioic acid *[111–20–6]*, **esters**
 esters, lubricants contg., for bearings and
  transmission, P 110342u
 esters with fatty acids and polyhydric alcs., prepn.
  of, for waxy carriers of perfumes for toilet
  deodorants, P 59761a
 mixed esters with glycerol, waste products,
  metalworking lubricants contg. amino paraffins
  and trichloroethylidenedisalicylic acid and, P
  146354p
 bis[2–[[3,5–bis(1,1–dimethylethyl)–4–◦
  hydroxyphenyl]thio]–1–methylethyl] ester
  [83913–08–0], antioxidants, for polyolefins, P
  5123a
•
•
•

 bis(2–ethylhexyl) ester *[122–62–3]*
  in borate fireproofing agent manuf., P 200849u
  coating with film contg., of steel, for corrosion
   prevention, P 165175x
  erasable marking inks contg., alc.–sol.
   polymer–based, P 18253t
  fluoro rubbersswelling in, heat aging effect on,
   216916z
  gas chromatog. stationary phase, soly. factors for,
   79012k
  gas evolution from irradiated, 223915b
  hydrolysis of, lubricity in relation to, 146172c
  liq.–membrane electrode contg., for blood pH
   detn. in humans, 122326e
  lubricating greases contg., for high–rpm
   machines, P 129042t
  lubricating oils, pressure–viscosity correlations of,
   modified Barus equation for, 110066g
  plasticized, for PVC, oxidn. of, binaphthalene
   dicarboxaldehyde derivs. effect on, 216464a
  plasticizers, for PVC, oxidn. of, binaphthalene
   dicarboxaldehyde deriv. effect on, 199146d
  plasticizers, PVC–nitrile rubber blends contg.,
   with improved resiliency and dimensional
   stability at high temp. and extrusion
   moldability, P 161778y
  plasticizers, in pyrotechnic compns. for neutral
   fog and smoke generation, P 218239e
  PVC plasticized with polypropylene glycol
   sebacate Bu ester and, oxidative thermal
   degrdn. of, 144376y
  sampling of aerosol, filter for, 148784c
  toxicity of, to HeLa cells, 12556x
  bis(2–ethylhexyl) ester, mixt. with
   tris(2–methylphenyl) phosphate
   [68337–07–5], hydrolysis of, lubricity in
   relation to, 146172c

Fig. 30: Excerpt from the Chemical Substance Index to Vol. 98

2.2 Sample search: What was published about the plasticizer DOS in
                    Volume 98 in 1983?
      To illustrate: Index Guide
                    Chemical Substance Index
                    Qualifiers
                    Categories

It can be assumed that the acronym DOS is derived from a trivial name.
However, even the trivial name, dioctylsebacic acid, provides no further help, as the CA Index Name of the substance is necessary for a
literature search. The Index Guide shows the inverted substance name
of DOS: decanedioic acid, esters, bis(2-ethylhexyl)ester (Fig. 29).

In the Chemical Substance Index to Chemical Abstracts, Vol. 98 (Fig.
30) the parent substance heading decanedioic acid can be found, then,
in round brackets, the trivial name commonly used in the literature.
The index entries and abstract numbers under decanedioic acid are
followed by topic-orientated subdivisions (qualifiers) and chemical-
function subdivisions (categories). The entry in the Index Guide shows
that abstracts about DOS are listed under the class of compound i.e.
esters of decanedioic acid. Under this index heading the individual
esters are named in alphabetical order. It is immediately obvious from
the text of the index entries that at least four publications dealing
with DOS as a plasticizer are abstracted in Vol. 98. Two of these
publications are patents, recognizable by the letter P preceding the
abstract number.

INDEX GUIDE–APPENDIX I

Health hazard 28ag, 54r, 56e
Health physics 28ag, 32b, 45q, 54r,
    56e
Hearing 4f, 28e
Heart 7e
Heart, disease or disorder 28b
Heart, neoplasm 28b
Heart, toxic chemical and physical
    damage 28b
Heat 28ae, 55c
Heat, biological effects 4g, 37f, 55c

Fig. 31: Excerpt from Appendix I of the Index Guide, the alphabetic
         list of subject terms used in the General Subject Index

2.3 Sample search: Is there an abstract on the subject of the drug
                    therapy of cardiac arrest in Volume 97 of Chemical
                    Abstracts?
   To illustrate: Alphabetical Hierarchy Index
                  Hierarchy of General Subject Headings
                  Qualifiers for Organs and Tissues
                  General Subject Index

The question makes no reference to any specific drug, but rather fo-
cusses on the physiological dysfunction of cardiac arrest.

The search begins in the Index Guide in order to ascertain the appropriate heading in the General Subject Index. However, there is no
reference to cardiac arrest. This means one of two things:

1. The term is very uncommon and thus not mentioned in the Index
   Guide. In this case a common, synonymous term should be sought.
2. The subject term has not been covered in the Chemical Abstracts.
How can one determine which of these situations apply?

Appendix I of the Index Guide contains two lists with all valid head-
ings in the General Subject Index: while the headings in the Hierarchy
Index are arranged alphabetically, those are in the Hierarchies of
General Subject Headings are grouped into 58 different subject areas.
These subject areas have nothing to do with the Sections in Chemical
Abstracts itself.

"Cardiac arrest" is not listed in the alphabetical Hierarchy Index
either. However, "heart" is synonymous with "cardiac", and this term
is included in the list (Fig. 31).

After "heart" with the code 7e the term is repeated several times followed by qualifying descriptions to show where it is used in specific
contexts, e.g. disease and disorder. The succeeding numbers refer to
the appropriate Hierarchy Subject Areas, the letter denotes the seg-
ment of the Subject Area in which the original term is to be found
(Fig. 32).

Hierarchy Subject Areas

Agriculture, 1
Analysis, 2
Animal cell, 3
Animal processes and phenomena, 4
Apparatus, 5
Biological pigments, 6
Body, animal, 7
Body fluid, 8
Building materials, 9
Catalysts and Catalysis, 10
Ceramic industry, 11
Electricity, 12
Electric property, 13
Elements, 14
Evolution and Genetics, 15
Food and Feed, 16
Functional groups, 17
Graphic arts, 18
Hormones, 19
Immunology, 20
Information science, 21
Inorganic compounds, 22
Kinetics, reaction, 23
Lipids, 24
Living systems, processes, and components, 25
Magnetic property, 26
Mechanics, 27
Medicine, 28
Metabolism, 29

Metallurgy, 30
Nuclear matter and phenomena, 31
Nuclear technology, 32
Organelle, 33
Organic compounds, 34
Particles, 35
Pharmaceuticals, 36
Plant, 37
Polymer additives, 38
Polymer applications, 39
Polymeric compositions, 40
Polymer processing, 41
Property, 42
Proteins, 43
Quantum mechanics, 44
Radiation, 45
Reaction, 46
Science, 47
Separation, 48
Soils, 49
Solids, 50
States of matter, 51
Structure, 52
Surface, 53
Technological processes and products, 54
Thermodynamics, 55
Toxicology, 56
Transport process and property, 57
Universe, 58

7. BODY, ANIMAL

(Anatomical part)
a • Abdomen
      • • Peritoneum
            •
            •
            •
            •
      • • Scale (anatomical)
e • • Scalp
      • • Sebaceous gland
      • • Sweat gland
      • • Wool
      • (System)
      • • Cardiovascular system
      • • • Blood vessel
      • • • • Artery
      • • • • Carotid sinus
      • • • • Capillary vessel
      • • • • Vein
→ • • • Heart
      • • • • Pericardium
      • • Digestive tract
      • • • Biliary tract

28. MEDICINE

a Andrology
    Disease
      • Cardiovascular system
            disease
      • • Blood pressure
            disorder
            •
            •
      • • Circulation
            disorder
b • • • Embolism
      • • • Hemorrhage
      • • • Hematoma
      • • • Hyperemia
      • • • Ischemia
      • • • Shock
      • • • Syncope
      • • • Thrombosis
      • • • Thrombus and Blood clot
→ • • Heart, disease or disorder
      • • • Heart, neoplasm
      • • • Heart, toxic chemical and physical
            damage
      • • Pericardium
            disease

Fig. 32: Excerpt from Appendix I of the Index Guide, subject terms in
         hierarchical order, divided into Hierarchy Subject Areas

Hierarchy Subject Group 7 deals with the subject area "body, animal". "Heart" appears as a more specific heading under the term "system". The brackets around the term "system" means that it is not an index heading. It may not be used in a search in the General Subject Index and has only been introduced into the hierarchical listing to eluci-date the systematic subdivision of the groups. The number of dots preceding each heading term designates the level of specificity: the more dots, the more specific the term.

Hierarchy Subject Area 28 shows the subdivisions of "medicine". "Heart, disease or disorder" is found as a specific term under the general headings of "disease" and "cardiovascular system". Publica-tions on the subject of cardiac arrest could be included under this heading, as Hierarchy Subject Areas 7 and 28 contain no further terms which are more closely related to the subject term expressed in the problem. Thus the search can proceed by consulting the heading "heart, disease or disorder" in the General Subject Index.

"Disease or disorder" is one of the index qualifiers, which subdivide comprehensive, subject-orientated headings in the General Subject Index. The following index qualifiers are for "Organ and Tissue" head-ings:
1. Composition
2. Disease or disorder
3. Metabolism
4. Neoplasm
5. Toxic, chemical and physical damage

VOL. 97, 1982 – GENERAL SUBJECT INDEX

Heart, disease or disorder
air pollution in relation to, in Pittsburgh,
        Pennsylvania, 77899k
in aluminum plant workers exposed to fluorides and
        fluorine, 114636v
in aluminum plant workers exposed to fluorine,
        114635u
amino(aryloxy)propanols as sympatholytics for
        treatment of, P 162606g
angina pectoris
    N–(aminoalkyl)dibenzoxazepinones for treatment
        of, P 182469t
    •
    •
    •
arrest
    in hypoxia in hypokinesia, adrenaline and Inderal
        effect on, 107939t
    as model for evaluation of antihypoxic drugs, in
        rat, 65909a
    potassium activity in, 89745v
    resuscitation from, inosine effect on, 174783a

Fig. 33: Excerpt from the General Subject Index to Vol. 97

Numerous abstracts dealing with "arrest" are listed under the heading "heart, disease or disorder" in the General Subject Index (Fig. 33). The text modifications indicate which of the publications shown here are relevant to the original question.

VOL 88, 1978 – CHEM. SUBSTANCE INDEX

Aspidospermidin-21-ol
—, 1-acetyl-17-methoxy-
(±)- *[58566-58-8]*, 23223f
acetate (ester), (±)- *[58566-59-9]*, total synthesis
of, 23223f
—, **17-methoxy-** *(cylindrocarpinol)* *[28189-98-2]*
mass spectra of, effect of ion source active sites on,
162457y
ASPK *[64900-31-8]*
friction of cutting tools from, on hardened steels
during turning, 26254c
Astatine *[7440-68-8]*
chem. of, R 28663j

Fig. 34: Excerpt from the Chemical Substance Index to Vol. 88

1977–INDEX GUIDE

Acetylsalicylic acid
See *Benzoic acid, 2-(acetyloxy)-* [50-78-2]
•
•
•

Salicylic acid acetate
See *Benzoic acid, 2-(acetyloxy)-* [50-78-2]

Fig. 35: Excerpt from the 1977 Index Guide

2.4 Sample search: Is there any reference to the effects of aspirin on
                    the aggregation of blood platelets in Vol. 88 of
                    Chemical Abstracts?
    To illustrate: Index Guide
                   Chemical Substance Index
                   CAS Registry Number
                   Text modifications

In recent years research into the effects of aspirin has increased due
to evidence of its implication in the possible prevention of heart
attacks.

The Chemical Substance Index contains no reference to the term aspirin
(Fig. 34). However, it would be wrong to conclude that no publication
about aspirin is included in this volume of Chemical Abstracts. Aspirin is only a trivial name, the drug is also known by a number of
chemical designations, e.g. acetylsalicylic acid, salicylic acid acetate or 2-(acetyloxy)benzoic acid. Which of these is the systematic
Index Name? This information is obtained from the Index Guide (Fig.
35). In the Chemical Substance Index it can be found under the name
benzoic acid, 2-(acetyloxy)-. Cross-references also lead from the
semi-systematic names to the inverted CA Index Name which is always
accompanied by the CAS Registry Number 50-78-2 in square brackets.

CHEMICAL ABSTRACTS - VOL. 88, 1978

Benzoic acid,

——, 2-(acetyloxy)- *(salicylic acid acetate)*
    [50-78-2] P 152253q
absorption and elimination of, after Doleron
    administration, age in relation to, 110447a
acetaminophen interaction with, 15715c
acetyl-CoA-decarboxylase of liver response to,
    31989a
aciphenoquinoline potentiometric detn. in
    pharmaceuticals in relation to, 94889p
ADPase of aorta potentiation by, 102110v
adsorption of
    by activated charcoal, 11840s, 163977e
    by mercury electrode, inhibiting properties in
    relation to, 13508p
    •

    •

of blood and synovial fluid, 182326h
blood platelet adhesion to activated charcoal and
    dialysis membranes response to, 68976v
blood platelet aggregation and deposition inhibition
    by, on thrombogenic surface, 98957g
blood platelet aggregation and prostaglandin
    formation inhibition by, pranoprofen in
    relation to, 182655q
blood platelet aggregation and secretionresponse to,
    Acinetobacter endotoxin in relation to,
    84325n
blood platelet aggregation in diabetes in response
    to, 18635n

● blood platelet aggregation inhibition by
    99285y
    carboxyl group effect on, 178f
    citrate and heparin effect on, 146179d
    dipyridamole in releation to, 499m
blood platelet aggregation response to
    98990n
    proquazone in relation to, 83526s
    ticlopidine interaction with, 146322v
blood platelet function response to, in stroke and
    transient ischemic attacks, 16134z
blood platelet nucleotide content and release in
    response to, 59823r
blood platelet secretion of granule constituents
    response to, 16667a
blood serum constituent detn. in presence of,
    185616p
    •

    •

    •

→ hypotension and inflammation inhibition by, blood
    platelet aggregation and prostaglandin
    synthetase in relation to, R 182110h
identification of, by IR spectroscopy, 177267k

Fig. 36: Excerpt from the Chemical Substance Index to Vol. 88

88: 99285y Inhibition of platelet aggregation in subjects treated with acetylsalicylic acid. Avellone, G.; Davi, G.; Di Liberti, M.; Riolo, F. P. (Ist. Patol. Med., Univ. Palermo, Palermo, Italy). *Boll. Soc. Ital. Cardiol.* **1976,** 21(12), 2101–6 (Ital). A single oral dose of *acetylsalicylic acid* (I) [50–78–2] to

humans either inhibited or completely abolished the aggregation of their platelets in vitro, as detd. by the collagen method of Born and the method of Breddin. There were considerable interindividual differences, with respect to both the degree of inhibition and its duration.

Fig. 37: Abstract from Vol. 88

In the Chemical Substance Index systematic substance names are supplemented by a common semi-systematic name followed by the CAS Registry
Number (Fig. 36). Subsequently, there is a long list of text modifications extracted from the abstract texts or the source literature. All
these text modifications should be carefully scanned to ensure that
the subject of blood platelets is not overlooked when it occurs in the
middle of a text modification (in Fig. 36 indicated by the arrow).

Numerous text modifications, however, begin with the term "blood
platelets". The text modification "blood platelets aggregation inhibition by 2-(acetyloxy)benzoic acid" corresponds very closely to the
original question.

When the abstract itself is consulted, it is evident that the CA Index
Name for aspirin is not used, but rather the designation the author
has used in his publication. However, the inclusion of both the structural formula and the CAS Registry Number leaves no doubt that this
paper deals with aspirin.

1982 INDEX GUIDE

Fischer–Tropsch synthesis
   See
        Hydrogenation
           of carbon monoxide
        Carbon monoxide [630–08–0], reactions
           hydrogenation of

Fig. 38: Excerpt from the 1982 Index Guide

2.5 Sample search: Does Chemical Abstracts, Vol.98 contain abstracts
                    about the Fischer-Tropsch synthesis?
    To illustrate: Index Guide
                   General Subject Index
                   Chemical Substance Index

The following shows a simplified version of the reactions occurring in
the Fischer-Tropsch synthesis:

$$C \quad + \quad H_2O \longrightarrow \quad CO \quad + \quad H_2$$

$$CO \quad + \quad H_2O \xrightarrow{\text{catalyst}} \quad \begin{array}{l} \text{Hydrocarbons} \\ \text{Alcohols} \\ \text{Aldehydes} \\ \text{Ketones} \end{array}$$

In this process steam is passed over coke at high temperature to yield
"synthesis gas", from which, using specific catalysts, a number of
products are obtained amongst which aliphatic hydrocarbons predomi-
nate. Small amounts of oxygen-containing compounds are also formed.

There are two references to the Fischer-Tropsch synthesis in the Index
Guide (Fig. 38). The "see" cross-references indicate that the term
Fischer-Tropsch synthesis is not itself a General Subject Heading.

The subsequent cross-references direct the searcher to:
1. Search under the heading "hydrogenation" in the General Subject Index, and in particular under the "hydrogenation of carbon monoxide". The term deals with a reaction or a process in this case.
2. Search in the Chemical Substance Index under "carbon monoxide", and
   in particular in the subgroup "reactions" and then specifically
   under "hydrogenation".

It is particularly important to gather a large number of search terms
which are closely related to the search topic when carrying out a
literature search about a subject as extensive as the Fischer-Tropsch
synthesis in order to ensure that even publications which do not include the term Fischer-Tropsch synthesis, but report results of research on this reaction, are also found. In both manual and computer-
assisted searches compiling search terms is the most important step,
as this is the development of a search profile. Once again the Index
Guide is indispensable for this purpose, and every search, whether
online or manual, should start with the Index Guide.

1982 INDEX GUIDE

Hydrogenation
See also *Reduction*
catalysts——see *Hydrogenation catalysts*
cracking and——see *Hydrocracking*
enthalpy of——see *Heat of hydrogenation*
kinetics of——see also *Kinetics of hydrogenation*
in methanation——see *Methanation*
• in petroleum refining——see *Petroleum refining*
•
•
•

Methanation
See also *Fuel gas manufacturing*
catalysts——see *Methanation catalysts*
enthalpy of——see *Heat of methanation*
kinetics of——see also *Kinetics of methanation*

Fuel gas manufacturing
See also *Methanation*
ammonia or gas liquors from——see *Ammonia liquor*
ammonia recovery from
see
　Ammonia [7664-41-7], preparation
　Sulfuric acid diammonium salt [7783-20-2], preparation
coke ovens for——see *Coke ovens*
gasification, of coal——see *Coal gasification*
of substitute or synthetic natural gas——see *Natural gas, substitute*

Fig. 39: Excerpt from the 1982 Index Guide

The term "hydrogenation" leads to further search concepts included in the controlled vocabulary of the Index Guide (Fig. 39). The first cross-reference under "hydrogenation" is "see also". In contrast to the reference "see", the "see also" reference means that both terms, in this case "hydrogenation" and "reduction", belong to the controlled vocabulary and are headings in the General Subject Index. The reference "see also" usually indicates the more general term which is higher in the hierarchy. Only the searcher can decide whether the more general term is relevant to his problem or not.

The term "reduction" is too general with regard to the Fischer-Tropsch synthesis and can therefore be ignored. The subsequent terms of cross-reference must be evaluated carefully for their relevance to the search question. The terms "hydrocracking" and "petroleum refining" are irrelevant to the Fischer-Tropsch synthesis. However, the remaining headings seem to be pertinent and should be included in the list of search terms.

"Methanation" is a particularly characteristic term for the Fischer-Tropsch synthesis. The Index Guide offers four further search terms under "methanation" (Fig. 39). The cross-reference to "fuel gas manufacturing" provides no new terms about the subject Fischer-Tropsch synthesis, rather a cross-reference leads back to "methanation".

The search terms determined up till now define the Fischer-Tropsch synthesis very well:
1. Hydrogenation of carbon monoxide
    2. Heat of hydrogenation
    3. Hydrogenation catalysts
    4. Kinetics of hydrogenation
    5. Methanation
        6. Heat of methanation
        7. Kinetics of methanation
        8. Methanation catalysts
        9. Fuel gas manufacturing
These terms deal only with subjects and are thus only suitable for searching in the General Subject Index. It is immaterial in which order the terms are looked up.

VOL. 98, 1983 – GENERAL SUBJECT INDEX

Hydrogenation
of (acetamidovinylthio)oxoazabicycloheptenecar=
  boxylate derivs., P 71802x
of acetic anhydride, ethylidene diacetate from, P
  142979y
of acetophenone on platinum, mechanism of,
  16155p
of acetylene
  ethene and propene on metal oxides, mechanism
    of, 34073q
  on silica–supported nickel, mechanism of,
    178502b
 •
 •
 •
of carbon monoxide
  R 92010c
  activation on metal surfaces in, R 218252d
  adsorbed on magnesia, adsorbed formaldehyde
    from, 22910x
  alcs. and hydrocarbon gases from, P 106792y
  alkylation of benzene and, in presence of tungsten
    carbonyl complexes, 34318y
  arom. hydrocarbon prepn. by, P 182502u
  evaluation of Fischer–Tropsch reactors for,
    128992r
  in Fischer–Tropsch process, slurry reactors for,
    128865b
  in Fischer–Tropsch process for fuels manuf. in
    South Africa, 146273m
  in Fischer–Tropsch reaction, economics and
    industrial processes of, R 74929e
  by Fischer–Tropsch synthesis, R 18984g
  in Fischer–Tropsch synthesis, chain growth and
    olefin in corporation in, 163682m
  in Fischer–tropsch synthesis, in gasoline manuf., P
    56892h
  in Fischer–Tropsch synthesis, prepn. of C_{2-4}
    hydrocarbons by, 163681k
  in Fischer–Tropsch synthesis, process
    optimization of, 218473b
  in Fischer–Tropsch synthesis, in prodn. of
    hydrocarbons, R 92026n
  in iron chloride graphite intercalate, Moessbauer
    spectra in relation to, 25135j
  in manuf. of paraffins, P 74243b
  mechanism of, R 88420u, R 88421v
  mechanism of catalytic, 34061j, 178438k,
    182394k
  mechanism of rhodium–catalyzed, 52849b
  for methanol, detn. of criteria of thermal stability
    of, 56376t
  methylene intermediate for, 106733e
  model reaction for elementary step of, 54186g
  in prodn. of gasoline, R 146088e
  in Sasol process, in prodn. of diesel fuel and
    gasoline, R 92025m
  in slurry bed in Fischer–Tropsch synthesis,
    product anal. in, 37393e
  sorption heats and crystallite size and support in
    relation to, 37248m
of carbon monoxide and carbon dioxide on rhodium,
  mechanism of, 106628z

of carbon monoxide in Fischer–Tropsch process,
  gasoline and diesel fuel prodn. by, R 182123w
of carbon monoxide in Fischer–Tropsch reaction,
  catalyst–sprayed tube wall reactors in,
  110272w
of carbon monoxide in Fischer–Tropsch reaction at
  low conversion, reaction products and effects
  of reactive scavengers in, 163697v
of carbon monoxide in Fischer–Tropsch syntheses, in
  South Africa, R 18999r
of carbon monoxide in Fischer–Tropsch synthesis
  alcs. from, manuf. of fuel extenders from, P
    6299z
  alkene selectivity of, R 18993j
  chain growth modeling of product distributions
    in, 110275z
  chromatog. anal. of products in, 163653c
  coal gasification requirements in, 56824n
  effect of potassium promoters on, 6281n
  forced–feed compn. cycling in, 37251g
  gas purifn. and sepn. in, R 56627a
  on–line gas–chromatog. method for anal. and
    products from, 110271v
  selective processes for, R 92033n
  selectivity of, in comparison with
    methanol–zeolite conversions, 19232x
of carbon monoxide in Fischer–Tropsch synthesis on
  supported ruthenium, effect of potassium
  promotion on, 37396h
of carbon monoxide in prepn. of alkanepolyol, P
  16275c
of carbon monoxide in prepn. of alkanepolyols, P
  4283r, P 4284s
of carbon monoxide in prepn. of ethylene glycol, P
  4285t
of carbon monoxide in prepn. of methanol, P
  142950g
of carbon monoxide in presence of propionic acid,
  alkyl propionate from, 125169s
of carbon monoxide on cobalt, mechanism of,
  52947g
of carbon monoxide on iron–alumina, mechanism of,
  106623u
of carbon monoxide on iron or iron–ruthenium,
  mechanism of, 106624v
of carbon monoxide on ruthenium, mechanism of,
  106592h
of carbon monoxide on supported rhodium, effect of
  supports on, 106625w
of carbon monoxide or copper oxide–zinc oxide,
  mechanism of, 52915v
of carbon monoxide over nickel, effect of potassium
  promoter on, 142768d
of carbon monoxide over unreduced iron oxides,
  mechanism of, 106621s
of carbon monoxide to methanol and higher alcs., P
  74251c
of carbon oxides, in methane synthesis by solid–state
  ionic method, 128967m

Fig. 40: Excerpt from the General Subject Index to Vol. 98

In the General Subject Index a large number of text modifications and abstract numbers are listed under the term "hydrogenation of carbon monoxide" (Fig. 40). Some text modifications contain the term "Fischer-Tropsch", for although "Fischer-Tropsch synthesis" is not part of the controlled vocabulary, it can occur in the index entries when the author used it in his original publication. All the abstracts in Fig. 40 about carbon monoxide could deal with the Fischer-Tropsch synthesis and should therefore be read. (The repetition of "of carbon monoxide" at the end of the listing has no significance to the content, it is only to enhance the legibility and clarity of the index. In the volume indexes the index entry is repeated when more than 30 abstracts are listed on the subject, in the collective indexes from 50 abstracts upwards. The prepositions are not taken into account when the entries are alphabetized.)

VOL. 98, 1983 – GENERAL SUBJECT INDEX

Heat of hydrogenation
of arenes, calcn. of, 88587d
of boron–nitrogen unsatd. compds., MNDO calcn.
of, 167238u
of silicon trihydride cation, comparison with carbon
trihydride cation, 167292g
Heat of hydrogen bonding
in acetone complex with hydrogen chloride, R
23158v

Fig. 41: Excerpt from the General Subject Index to Vol. 98

VOL. 98, 1983 – GENERAL SUBJECT INDEX

Hydrogenation catalysts
allylplatinum complexes, for alkadienes, 142765a
alumina supported copper, for Me linoleate, kinetics
and mechanism with, 215010n
•

•

•
for carbon monoxide
copper oxide, zinc oxide, and aluminum
isopropoxide–contg., P 197602a
mechanism with, R 88421v, 106733e
of carbon monoxide, tungsten carbonyl complex
catalysts, for alkylation of benzene, 34318y
carbonylation and, rhodium chloride and P compds.
as, for carboxylic anhydride, P 106812e
•

•

•
copper oxide–zinc oxide
for carbon monoxide, active species in reduced,
92229f
for carbon monoxide, mechanism of synergism in
methanol formation by, 52915v
copper–palladium, for dimethylethynylcarbinol,
178687r
copper–zinc
for carbon monoxide and carbon dioxide,
106626x
for carbon monoxide–carbon dioxide, P 4287v
•

•

•
contg. ferric oxide, for carbon monoxide in
Fischer–Tropsch process, 6147y
ferric oxide–tungsten oxide, for heavy oils from coal
liquefaction, P 110431x
for Fischer–Tropsch reaction, R 146110f
for Fischer–Tropsch synthesis
cobalt–palladium or cobalt–platinum, P 163811c
for olefin and diesel fuel selectivity, R 92033n

•

•

•
iron
alumina–supported, for Fisher–Tropsch
synthesis, potassium promotion of, 6281n
for carbon dioxide, mechanism with, 71281b
for carbon monoxide, conversion limits with,
106622t
iron/alumina, for carbon dioxide, 106627y
iron–alumina, for carbon monoxide, 106623u
contg. iron and another transition metal, supported,
for coal liquefaction, P 56978r
iron and manganese reduced oxides, carbon
deposition on, 204923m
iron carbonyl, for styrene, 16134f
iron–contg. zeolites, sodium chloride treatment
effect on, 222536s
iron–graphite, lamellar, for carbon monoxide in
Fischer–Tropsch synthesis, 56842s
•

•

•
nickel
for acetylene or ethylene, SIMS in relation to
mechanism with, 178544s
for alkylanthraquinones, 197417u
contg. alumina chromia, for alkoxydodecadiene, P
178819k
on brick support, for vegetable oils, P 36476x
for butynediol, P 160235g
for carbon monoxide, R 41326c
for carbon monoxide in Fischer–Tropsch
synthesis, hydrogen isotope and support
effects in presence of, 19115m

Fig. 42: Excerpt from the General Subject Index to Vol. 98

The second search term from the search profile "heat of hydrogenation" provides little additional information to the search (Fig. 41), more abstracts are found under "hydrogenation catalysts" (Fig. 42). The text modifications mainly describe the composition of the catalysts. All entries should therefore be critically examined to determine under which circumstances the various catalysts have been employed and studied.

VOL. 98, 1983 – GENERAL SUBJECT INDEX

Kinetics of hydrogenation
  of acetophenone on platinum, 16155p
  of acetylene, on silica–supported nickel catalysts,
      178502b
  of alkenes, catalytic, 52948h
  of alkenes in presence of cobalt carbonyls, 198410y
  of alkenoic acids in presence of rhodium complexes
      contg. bis(phosphino)ferrocenes, 215759p
  of alkylanthraquinones on nickel, model for,
      197417u
  of alkylbenzoic acids on ruthenium, 88602e
  of arenes, enthalpy of hydrogenation in relation to,
      88587d
  of arom. nitro compds., solvent and substituent
      effects on, 16154n
  of butadiene, on transition metal phosphide
      catalysts, 71430z
  of carbon dioxide, in presence of hydrogen–⊃
      permeable membrane catalysts, 167705u
  of carbon monoxide
    catalytic, 125120u
    evaluation of Fischer–Tropsch reactors for,
        128992r
    in Fischer–Tropsch process, 6281n
    in homogeneous system contg. ruthenium
        catalysts, 145408x

Fig. 43: Excerpt from the General Subject Index to Vol. 98

VOL. 98, 1983 – GENERAL SUBJECT INDEX

Kinetics of methanation
  of carbon dioxide, on nickel catalysts, 200904h
  of carbon dioxide on ruthenium, 37397j
  of carbon monoxide
    isotopic transients in relation to, 201114n
    on nickel catalysts, 182374d
  of coconut char, 53107v

Fig. 44: Excerpt from the General Subject Index to Vol. 98

Publications concerning the Fischer-Tropsch synthesis are also listed under the heading "kinetics of hydrogenation - of carbon monoxide" (Fig. 43). The term "kinetics of methanation" provides little relevant information (Fig. 44).

VOL. 98, 1983 – GENERAL SUBJECT INDEX

Methanation
  carbon deposition in, reactivity and removal of,
    110265w
  of carbon dioxide
   → over rhodium, preoxidn. effect on, 182398q
    solar thermochem. energy conversion and storage
     system based on, 163961b
  of carbon dioxide on ruthenium, mechanism of,
    37397j
  of carbon monoxide
    in manuf. of liq. methane, P 37504s
    mechanism of, 182374d
    mechanism of catalyzed, 218597v
 → ruthenium, effect of surface complexes on,
    56860w
  of carbon monoxide from catalytic methanol
    decomp., 218596u
  of carbon monoxide in aq. ruthenium suspensions, P
    129117w
  of carbon monoxide in hydrogen–poor synthesis gas,
    163668m
  of carbon monoxide on supported ruthenium, effect
    of potassium promotion on, 37396h
  by coal devolatilization, 2–stage gasification process
    for manuf. of high–Btu gases by, P 92443w
  of coal gas, by catalytic steam reforming, corrosion
    prevention by ammonia in, P 218758y
  in coal gasification, by Exxon process, R 109988c
  of coconut char, mechanism of, 53107v
  of coke–oven gas, process development for, R
    182091j
  heat transfer in, manuf. of superheated steam by, in
    manuf. of substitute natural gas, P 92453z
  of peat, 146283q
  in substitute natural gas prodn., in indirect coal
    liquefaction, simulation of, 110264v
  of synthesis gas, high–temp. catalytic, 110111t
Methanation catalysts
  for coke–oven gas, R 182091j
  hydro–, iron–nickel, 19212r
  iron carbide silicide, formation of, in fluidized–bed
    coal gasification, P 163807f
  •
  •
  •

nickel
  R 41326c
  activity and thermal stability of, calcination
    temp. effect on, 19257j
  for carbon monoxide, 182374d
  for carbon monoxide, hydrogen sulfide poisoning
    of, 182384g
  •
  •
  •

rhodium
 → for carbon dioxide, preoxidn. effect on, 182398q
 ✳ for carbon monoxide, support interaction in,
    186331k
ruthenium
  for carbon monoxide, support in relation to
    selectivity of, 6146x
  for carbon monoxide in hydrocarbon synthesis, P
    92458e
  prepn. and surface characteristics of, 186296c
ruthenium–alumina, for carbon monoxide, γ
    radiation in relation to sulfur poisoning of,
    201115p
ruthenium carbonyl cluster complexes,
    characterization of, B 60531g
ruthenium on silica–alumina or charcoal, for carbon
    monoxide in aq. suspensions, P 129117w
ruthenium–silica
 → carbon monoxide, formation of surface complexes
    on, 56860w
  for carbon monoxide, effect of potassium
    promotion on, 37396h
  stopped–flow chromatog. study of reactive sites
    on, 167678n
tetrairidium dodecacarbonyl–aluminum
    chloride–sodium chloride, for carbon monoxide
    in Fischer–Tropsch process, 218566j

Fig. 45: Excerpt from the General Subject Index to Vol. 98

During such a comprehensive search it is not uncommon to find several references to the same abstract, e.g. two abstracts about "methanation" are also listed under the heading "methanation catalysts" (Fig. 45). The heading, under which a publication is indexed, depends on which aspects of the subject matter the author has emphasized.

VOL. 98, 1983 – CHEM. SUBSTANCE INDEX

Carbon monoxide *[630-08-0]*, **reactions**
addn. reaction of
  to dodecacarbonylbis(μ_3–sulfido)tetraosmium,
    45861w
  with pentafluorophenyl nitrene, isocyanate by low
    temp., 88892z
  •
  •
  •
hydrogenation of
  R 92010c, P 110422v
  activity of molybdenum sulfide catalysts for,
    oxygen in relation to, 128961e
  adsorbed on magnesia, adsorbed formaldehyde
    from, 22910x
  alcs. and hydrocarbon gases from, P 106792y
  amorphous inorg. catalysts for, P 96476g
  arom. hydrocarbon prepn. by, P 182502u
  to C_{2-3} acids and esters, catalysts for, P 91408b
  catalysis and mechanism of, 110115x
  catalysts for, P 4287v, P 18464n, P 56014y, P
    74256h, 106626x, P 106823j, 125189y, P
    142957q
  catalysts for, in Fischer–Tropsch reaction,
    92216z
  catalysts for, in Fischer Tropsch synthesis,
    128966k
  •
  •
  •

evaluation of Fischer–Tropsch reactors for,
  128992r
in Fischer–Tropsch process, chain growth
  modeling of product distributions in, 110275z
in Fischer–Tropsch process, cobalt–palladium or
  cobalt–platinum catalysts for, P 163811c
in Fischer–Tropsch process, gasoline and diesel
  fuels prodn. from, R 182123w
in Fischer–Tropsch process, homogeneous
  catalysts for, kinetics and mechanism of,
  218566j
in Fischer–Tropsch process, slurry reactors for,
  128865b
in Fischer–Tropsch process for fuels manuf. in
  South Africa, 146273m
  •
  •
  •
in prodn. of gasoline, R 146088e
on rhodium, effect of catalyst support on,
  106625w
on rhodium catalysts, 106628z
* on rhodium supported catalyst, 186331k
on rhodium–tin catalysts, 60540j
on ruthenium, mechanism of, 106592h
ruthenium carbonyl–hydride complex catalyst
  for, 167699v
ruthenium–catalyzed, 200916p
over ruthenium–zeolite catalysts, olefin selectivity
  in, 200917q

Fig. 46: Excerpt from the Chemical Substance Index to Vol. 98

The search for subject-orientated terms concerning the Fischer-Tropsch synthesis will be abandoned here. The Index Guide also contains a cross-reference to the Fischer-Tropsch synthesis which leads to the Chemical Substance Index, namely the entry "carbon monoxide, reactions, hydrogenation of" (Fig. 46). The addition of "reactions" serves as a reminder that the abstracts about carbon monoxide are assigned to various subgroups by qualifiers and categories.

It is evident from scanning the text modifications in the Chemical Substance Index that many of the abstracts were mentioned in the General Subject Index. Duplication of references is an indication of the importance of a particular paper to the search problem – the more search terms which lead to the same abstract, the more relevant the publication is to the problem.

All the abstracts under a relevant heading should be consulted to ensure the completeness of a literature search, as the text modifications are selected according to the subject matter stressed by the author in his paper. His paper could well include aspects which are of interest for the search, but which are not the main topic of his publication. This additional information can be obtained only by reading the text of the abstract.

VOL. 88, 1978 – FORMULA INDEX

$C_2H_2Cl_2O$

Acetaldehyde, dichloro– *[79-02-7]*, 37077y, R
   120523m, 131632x

Acetyl chloride, chloro– *[79-04-9]*. See *Chemical Substance Index*

$C_2H_2Cl_2O_2$

Acetic acid, dichloro– *[79-43-6]*. See *Chemical Substance Index*
   compd. with [6R-[6α,7β(R*)]]–7–⊙
     [(aminophenylacetyl)amino]–3–methyl–8–⊙
     oxo–5–thia–1–azabicyclo[4.2.0]oct–2–ene–2–⊙
     carboxylic acid (1:1) *[66084-61-5]*, P 136632g
   compd. with 1–[4–[2–(diethylamino)ethoxy]–⊙
     3,5–dimethylphenyl]–3,3–diphenyl–1–⊙
     propanone (1:1) *[65083-80-9]*, P 37425k
   compd. with N–(1–methylethyl)–2–propanamine
     (1:1) *[660-27-5]*, 69312n, 69313p, 183072j
   compd. with N–(1–methylethyl)–2–⊙
     pyrimidinamine *[65567-05-7]*, 84054y
→ compd. with piperazine *[66398-51-4]*, P 182032j
   compd. with piperidine (1:1) *[66398-50-3]*, P
     182032j
   mercury(2+) salt *[26788-74-9]*, 88943k
● sodium salt *[2156-56-1]*, 44993x, 183129h
   telomer with carbon monoxide and ethene
     [66330-36-7], P 153263e
   tin(4+) salt *[66096-29-5]*, 145335g

$C_2H_2Cl_2O_4Ti$

Titanium, dichlorobis(formato–O)–
   (T–4)–, homopolymer *[66068-81-3]*, 163110s

Fig. 47: Excerpt from the Formula Index to Vol. 88

2.6 Sample search: What is the fastest method of finding abstracts
about the substance with the molecular formula:

$$\begin{array}{c} Cl \\ | \\ H-C-C \\ | \\ Cl \end{array} \begin{array}{c} {}^{\nearrow O} \\ {}_{\searrow ONa} \end{array}$$

To illustrate: Molecular formulae
Formula Index
Chemical Substance Index

According to the Hill System, the molecular formula of the above-mentioned substance is: $C_2HCl_2NaO_2$. However, it is not recorded under
this molecular formula in the Formula Index.

As a salt of an acid, the modified Hill System places it under the
molecular formula of the acid:

$$\begin{array}{c} Cl \\ | \\ H-C-C \\ | \\ Cl \end{array} \begin{array}{c} {}^{\nearrow O} \\ {}_{\searrow OH} \end{array}$$

The Formula Index initially gives the CA Index Name written in the
inverted form, followed by the CAS Registry Number in square brackets
(Fig. 47). The subsequent reference to the Chemical Substance Index
indicates that 20 or more abstracts about dichloroacetic acid are
listed there. (A similar reference in the collective indexes is given
when they contain more than 50 abstracts about the substance.)

VOL. 88, 1978 – CHEM. SUBSTANCE INDEX

Acetic acid, dichloro-, compounds
 cobalt complex *[38246-85-4]*, reactions of, with
   sodium selenite, 130069g
 compd.
   with [6*R*-[6α,7β(*R)]]-7-⌐**
     [(aminophenylacetyl)amino]-3-methyl-⌐
     8-oxo-5-thia-1-azabicyclo[4.2.0]oct-2-⌐
     ene-2-carboxylic acid (1:1) *[66084-61-5]*,
     pure cephalexin from, P 136632g
 •
 •
 •
 mercury complex *[64252-29-5]*, 88943k
 mercury(2+) salt *[26788-74-9]*, reaction of, with
   cyclohexenylmethoxyphenol, 88943k
 molybdenum complex *[66625-71-6]*, prepn. and
   spectra of, 200239p
 molybdenum complex *[66625-72-7]*, prepn. and
   spectra of, 200239p
 silver complex *[66083-46-3]*, 163031s
 sodium salt *[2156-56-1]*
   blood lactate response to, in hepatitis, 44993x
   lipid metab. response to, in diabetes and
     hyperlipoproteinemia, 183129h
 tin(4+) salt *[66096-29-5]*, 145335q
 titanium complex *[19126-53-5]*, 202305f

Fig. 48: Excerpt from the Chemical Substance Index to Vol. 88

The Formula Index primarily contains references to molecular addition compounds or salts. The Chemical Substance Index must be consulted to ascertain in which context the particular substance was mentioned in the cited literature (Fig. 48). The sodium salt of the dichloroacetic acid is found under the subdivision "compounds". This subheading is described in the definition of categories (cf. 2.1.3, pp. 31 and 32). The text modifications following the individual compounds provide information about the contents of the publication.

VOL. 88, 1978 – FORMULA INDEX

C₄H₁₀N₂

Piperazine *[110-85-0]*. See *Chemical Substance Index*
bis(O,O–dioctadecyl phosphorodithioate)
 [66165-41-1], P 137704u
bis(2–hydroxypropanoate) *[64822-10-2]*, 15700u
compd. with arsenic acid (H₃AsO₄) (1:1)
 [66034-18-2], 190624u
compd. with 4–butyl–1,2–diphenyl–3,5–
 pyrazolidinedione (1:1) *[4985-25-5]*, 58543n,
 98990n, 99004f, 146037f
compd. with 4–butyl–1–phenyl–2–(4–phenyl–
 2–thiazolyl)–3,5–pyrazolidinedione (1:1)
 [66181-61-1], P 152613g
compd. with 5–chloro–N–(2–chloro–4–
 nitrophenyl)–2–hydroxybenzamide
 [34892-17-6], 44766a, 164034g, 164363p,
 164366s
compd. with N–(2,6–dimethylphenyl)–1,2–
 dihydro–2–oxo–3–pyridinecarboxamide
 [66009-85-6], P 141691e
compd. with N–(2,6–dimethylphenyl)–1,2–
 dihydro–2–oxo–3–pyridinecarboxamide (1:1)
 [65675-08-3], P 110533a
compd. with molybdic acid *[65125-43-1]*, P
 51574q
compd. with molybdic acid (H₂MoO₄) (2:1)
 [52364-65-5], P 38576x
compd. with 3–(sulfooxy)estra–1,3,5(10)–
 trien–17–one (1:1) *[7280-37-7]*, 32454j
compd. with 2,3,5,6–tetrachloro–1,4–benzenediol
 (1:1) *[65037-38-9]*, 21479v
decanedioate (1:1), polymer with
 1,6–hexanediamine hexanedioate (1:1) and
 piperazine nonanedioate (1:1) *[66027-30-3]*, P
 137616s
diacetate *[7204-34-4]*, 15700u
dichloroacetate *[66398-51-4]*, P 182032j
dihydriodide *[58464-47-4]*, 159234t
dihydrochloride *[142-64-3]*. For general derivs.
 see *Chemical Substance Index*
(diphosphate) (1:1) *[66034-17-1]*, 190624u
L–glutamate (1:1) *[66034-16-0]*, 190624u
hexanedioate (1:1) *[142-88-1]*, 99211w
(3β,20β)–3–hydroxy–11–oxoolean–12–en–3–t–
 29–oate *[65175-51-1]*, P 38003h
mixt. contg. *[63514-11-4, 66424-23-5,
 66424-25-7]*, 44766a, 182585s

Fig. 49: Excerpt from the Formula Index to Vol. 88

Fig. 47 shows a typical example of the indexing policy to facilitate the identification of the salts of amines. Here a compound (marked by the arrow), which is normally listed under piperazine, is mentioned under dichloroacetic acid. The full systematic name of the substance is found under the amine, piperazine $C_4H_{10}N_2$ (Fig. 49). According to the indexing rules all salts of amines, with the exception of those of the common acids like hydrochloric, nitric and sulphuric acids, are listed under the molecular formula (in the Formula Index) or the name (in the Chemical Substance Index) of both the acid and the amine components.

Vol. 91 Numerical Patent Index

SWISS

NO.	REF.
601224	20304j
608156	142040r
318	212541f
609053	39316m
084	92981a
210	57023t
243	27190c
443	6861g
473	30511p
560	27191d
712	74784j
713	20908j

Fig. 50: Excerpt from the Numerical Patent Index to Vol. 91

Vol. 91 Patent Concordance

SWISS

PATENT NUMBER	CORRESPONDING PATENT		CA REF. NUMBER
609337	Ger	2514937	
609338	Ger	2735431	
609340	Ger	2354002	
609342	Ger	2408804	
609349	Ger	2630474	
609350	Ger	2428139	
609356	Ger	2508082	

Fig. 51: Excerpt from the Patent Concordance to Vol. 91

2.7 Sample search: What are the contents of the two Swiss patents,
nos. 609210 and 609340?

To illustrate: Numerical Patent Index
Patent Concordance
Patent Index

In order to illustrate the Numerical Patent Index and the Patent Concordance, which were both issued until 1981, this search will be initially carried out in the volume index to Chemical Abstracts, Vol. 91.
Patent number 609210 with the appropriate abstract number is listed in
the Numerical Patent Index under "Swiss", but patent number 609340 is
not mentioned (Fig. 50). The Numerical Patent Index only includes
patents which were abstracted in that particular volume of Chemical
Abstracts (or in the appropriate collective period). Patents belonging
to a patent family are listed in the Patent Concordance. Therefore, if
a patent number is not found in the Numerical Patent Index, the Patent
Concordance must be consulted.

The Patent Concordance, which is arranged according to the alphabetical order of the countries, shows the second Swiss patent without a CA
abstract number, but with a reference to an equivalent German patent
(Fig. 51).

Vol. 91 Patent Concordance

GERMAN

PATENT NUMBER	CORRESPONDING PATENT		CA REF. NUMBER
2354001	Belg	821474	83: 98494a
	Brit	1483493	
	Fr	2249122	
	Jpn K	75 74651	
	Neth	7413997	
	Swiss	611321	
	US	4056508	
2354002	Aust	335076	83: 97678b
	Aust	335631	
	Aust	335632	
	Aust	335633	
	Aust	335634	
	Aust	336202	
	Belg	821505	
	Brit	1482552	
	Can	1056377	
	Fr	2248838	
	Jpn K	75 71679	
	Neth	7413980	
	S Afr	74 06790	
	Swiss	609046	
	Swiss	609047	
	Swiss	609048	
→	Swiss	609340	
	Swiss	609685	
	Swiss	609686	
	US	3981874	
	US	4038397	

Fig. 52: Excerpt from the Patent Concordance to Vol. 91

Fig. 52 shows the entire patent family and the appropriate abstract number of the German patent, which appeared in Vol. 83. The patent family was extended by the Swiss patent, number 609340, in Vol. 91.

91: 57023t Insecticidal and acaricidal triazolothiazolol phosphates (phosphonates). Hoffmann, Hellmut; Stendel, Wilhelm; Hammann, Ingeborg; Behrenz, Wolfgang (Bayer A.-G.) **Swiss 609,210** (Cl. A01N9/36), 28 Feb 1979, Ger. Appl. 2,350,631, 09 Oct 1973; 10 pp. Insecticidal and acaricidal

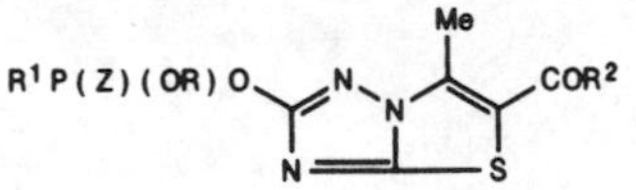

I (R = C_{1-6} alkyl; R^1 = C_{1-4} alkyl, C_{1-6} alkoxy, Ph; R^2 = alkyl- or dialkylamino, C_{1-6} alkoxy; Z = O, S] were prepd. Thus, 2-carbomethoxy-3-methyl-6-hydroxy-[1,2,4]-triazolo[3,2-b]thiazole reacted with $(EtO)_2P(S)Cl$ to give I (R = Et, R^1 = EtO, R^2 = OMe, Z = S), which (0.001% soln.) gave 100% control of *Myzus persicae*.

Fig. 53: Abstract from Vol. 91

97678b N-(Methoxymethylfurylmethyl)-6,7-benzomorphans and -morphinans. Merz, Herbert; Langbein, Adolf; Walther, Gerhard; Stockhaus, Klaus (Boehringer, C. H., Sohn) **Ger. Offen. 2,354,002** (Cl. C07D, A61K), 07 May 1975, Appl. P 23 54 002.5, 27 Oct 1973; 48 pp. Benzomorphans I (R = R^5,R^6; R^1

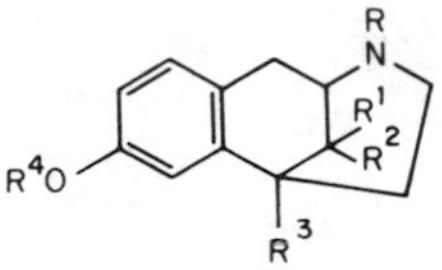

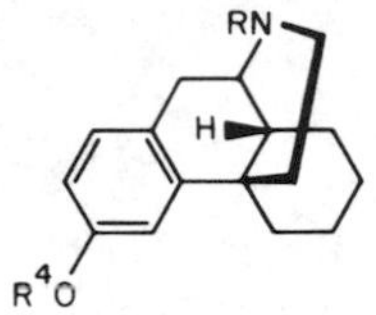

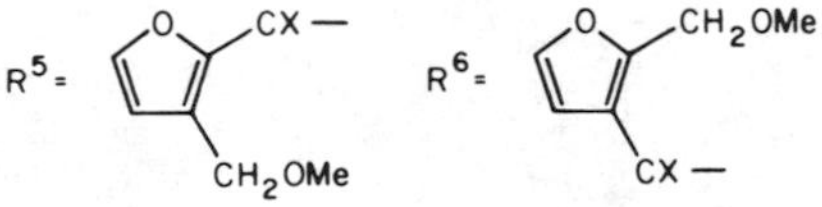

= H, Me, Et, R^2 = H; R^1 = R^2 = Me; R^3 = H, Me, Et, Pr; R^4 = H, Me, Ac; X = O, H_2) (22 compds.) and their salts, useful as analgesics (no data), and morphinans II (R = R^5, R^6; R^4 = H; X = O, H_2) were prepd. in 39–90% yield by alkylation of I and II (R = H) with R^5Cl and R^6Cl (X = H_2) or by acylation of I and II (R = H) with R^5Cl and R^6Cl (X = O) followed by redn. with $LiAlH_4$. Thus, I (R = R^2 = R^4 = H, R^1 = R^3 = Me) treated with R^6Cl (X = H_2) gave 88.5% I (R = R^6; R^1 = R^3 = Me; R^2 = R^4 = H, X = H_2) isolated as methanesulfonate.

Fig. 54: Abstract from Vol. 83

The title of a patent abstract is often not identical to that of the
patent itself, since patent titles are often deliberately expressed in
very vague and general terms. However, the title of an abstract should
be informative and the Chemical Abstracts Service attempts to outline
the contents of the patent in the patent heading (Fig. 53 and 54).

As the tenth collective period of Chemical Abstracts is complete and
the collective index for Vols. 86 to 95 (1977 to 1981) has been issued, the same search can be carried out more rapidly in the new Patent Index. This index combines the information contained in the Numerical Patent Index and the Patent Concordance. It is the aim of the
Patent Index to present, in the broadest sense, the patent family to
which each of the listed patents belongs. The degree to which the
patents are related to each other is indicated by the addition of such
phrases as "related", non-priority", "continuation in part".

1977–1981 PATENT INDEX

CH (Switzerland)

→ 609210 A, *See* DE 2350631 A1
609211 A, *See* NL 75/03001 A
609215 A, *See* DE 2621868 A1
609216 A, *See* DE 2456356 A1
609217 A, 90:148708r
609218 A, *See* DE 2527569 A1
609239 A, *See* DE 2404073 A1

•

•

609336 A, *See* US 3892776 A
609337 A, *See* DE 2514937 A1
609338 A, *See* DE 2735431 A1
609339 A, *See* DE 2416295 A1
→ 609340 A, *See* DE 2354002 A1
609341 A, *See* DE 2654797 A1

DE (Germany, Federal ...)

2350631 A1 (C2), 83:58834e
    AT 326690 B
    BE 820764 A1
    BR 74/08314 A0
    CA 1048034 A1
→   CH 609210 A, 91:57023t
    CS 178932 P
    DD 116045 C
    DK 134913 B
    ES 430786 A1
    FR 2246565 B1
    GB 1437055 A
    HU 169649 P
    JP 50/064292 A2

•

•

•

2354002 A1, 83:97678b
    AT 335631 B
    AT 335632 B
    AT 335633 B
    AT 335076 B
    AT 336202 B
    AT 335634 B
    BE 821505 A1
    CA 1056377 A1
    CH 609046 A
    CH 609047 A
    CH 609048 A
→   CH 609340 A
    CH 609685 A
    CH 609686 A
    CS 171194 P
    CS 171195 P
    CS 171196 P
    DD 115909 C
    DK 138325 C
    ES 431054 A1
    ES 431055 A1
    ES 431056 A1
    ES 431057 A1
    ES 431058 A1
    ES 431059 A1
    FR 2248838 A1
    GB 1482552 A
    HU 18834 O (176479 P)
    JP 50/071679 A2

Fig. 55: Excerpt from the Patent Index to the 10th collective period

Both Swiss patent numbers 609210 and 609340 are listed under CH, the
abbreviated symbol for the country (Fig. 55). Beside each of them
there is a cross-reference to the equivalent German patent. The patent
family is shown under DE, the abbreviation for the Federal Republic of
Germany. In this case it is possible to recognize at a glance that an
abstract of Swiss patent number 609210 appeared in Vol. 91, although
the related German patent, number 2350631, had already been abstracted
in Vol. 83. Thus, the patents emphasize different aspects of the same
basic invention.

1982–1986 INDEX GUIDE

Piceol
   See *Ethanone, 1-(4-hydroxyphenyl)- [99-93-4]*

Fig. 56: Excerpt from the Index Guide to the 11th collective period

1982–1986 CHEM. SUBSTANCE INDEX

Ethanone,

——, **1-(4-hydroxyphenyl)-** *[99-93-4]*, **97**: 55717x,
        P 215756q; **98**: 122875h; **102**: 24191p; **103**:
        37145x; **104**: P 109223s
acetylation of, **105**: 97363t
acidity of, in gas vs. soln. phases, LFER for, **100**:
        174190k
activity of, in gas chromatog. stationary phases at
        infinite diln., **97**: 134386s
acylation of
    with glyoxylic acid, **99**: P 70390v
    phase–transfer catalysis in, **101**: 191443h
adsorption of, by activated carbon, from water,
        purifn. in relation to, **105**: 84840w
Agrobacterium tumefaciens virulence gene
        expression activation by, **104**: 85553w
alkenylation of, by hexafluoropropene trimer, **104**: P
        207286j
alkylation of
    by azidobutyrate, **96**: 143281k
    by chlorobutene, **102**: 166098n
    by (phenylthio)alkyl bromides and chlorides, **99**:
        121910z

Fig. 57: Excerpt from the Chemical Substance Index to the 11th collec-
        tive period

2.8 Sample search: Carry out a comprehensive search for literature
concerning the substance piceol.

To illustrate: Index Guide
Collective Chemical Substance Indexes from the
eleventh to the first collective period

Regardless of whether the molecular formula or the systematic CA Index
Name of this substance is known or not, the latest Index Guide should
initially be consulted (Fig. 56). The systematic substance name for
piceol is 1-(4-hydroxyphenyl)ethanone in the Index Guide to the eleventh collective period. The name is written in the inverted form in
the Index Guide to facilitate easier access to the entry in the Chemical Substance Index (Fig. 57) during the search. Besides the name, the
CAS Registry Number, 99-93-4, is also given, and should be noted when
carrying out such a comprehensive search, as it can serve as a useful
verification if the systematic substance name has been changed as a
result of a nomenclature revision.

1977–1981 INDEX GUIDE

Piceol
See *Ethanone, 1–(4–hydroxyphenyl)– [99–93–4]*

1977–1981 CHEM. SUBSTANCE INDEX

Ethanone,

——, **1-(4-hydroxyphenyl)-** *[99–93–4]*, **86:** 5070h;
      88: P 37427n; **92:** 198060k; **94:** 191029q
acidity of, **92:** 110342v
acylation of
      92: 215016v
      with acryloyl and methacryloyl chloride, catalysts
            for, **94:** 174571t
O–acylation of, phase–transfer catalyzed, **93:**
      185890b
addn. and elimination reaction of, with
      sulfonyldiimidazole, **93:** 46510q
adsorbed, tunneling in study of, **90:** 175196d
adsorption of, by Sehadex, **89:** 153242t
from *Agastachys odorata*, **92:** 143221h
N–alkylanilino derivs., oxidn. of, electrochem., **86:**
      80819n
alkylation of, **88:** 62098p
O–alkylation of
      87: 33431r; **90:** 376k
      by 1–bromooctane, **89:** P 23969z
      by methoxyethyl bromide, **95:** P 168821d
      by α–phthalimidobutyrolactone, **91:** 123590d
      by trifluoroethyl mesylate, **94:** 83707a
from *Artemesia campestris*, **94:** 171016e

Fig. 58: Excerpt from the Index Guide and Chemical Substance Index to
          the 10th collective period

Prior to Vol. 96, i.e. the period 1977 to 1981, the Tenth Collective Index can be used for the search. Piceol is once again entered under the systematic name of 1-(4-hydroxyphenyl)-ethanone (Fig. 58) in the Index Guide to the tenth collective period. In the collective indexes the abstract numbers are necessarily preceded by the CA volume numbers (in boldface type). References to abstract numbers without text modifications are found in the Chemical Substance Index following the inverted CA Index Name and the CAS Registry Number (Fig. 58). These abstracts only report on preparation or synthesis. If the author had given additional information about purification methods or, for instance, about further reactions that particular entry would contain a text modification in the index.

9th COLL.   INDEX GUIDE

Piceol
   See *Ethanone, 1-(4-hydroxyphenyl)- [99-93-4]*

9th COLL.   1972-1976 CHEM. SUBSTANCE INDEX

Ethanone

——, 1-(4-**hydroxyphenyl**)- *[99-93-4]*, **76:** 112843c;
        78: 135815a; **79:** 136735g; **81:** 49378r; **82:**
        3897b; **84:** P 164449p
   as acetophenone or ethylbenzene metabolite, in
        urine, **81:** 164022g
   activators, for styrene polymer degradation by light,
        77: P 49471h
   addn. of, to aryl vinyl sulfones, kinetics of, **80:**
        59155j
   addn. reaction of, with hydroxylamine, **76:** 98663k
   addn. reaction with hydroxylamine, kinetics and
        mechanism of, **85:** 93343g
   adsorption of
        by activated alumina, solvent effect on, **81:**
           6469d
        on silica gel, **79:** 10212r
   aldol condensation of, **84:** P 16961j
   of *Apocynum venetum*, **76:** 32232n
   Baeyer–Villiger reaction of, kinetics of, **77:** 139232k
   benzoylation of, with triethylamine catalysts,
        kinetics of, **80:** 47066t
   biodegrdn. of, by Pseudomonas ovalis, **84:** 61523d
   bromination and chlorination of, **85:** P 177068j
   bromination of
        with cupric bromide, **85:** 177007p

Fig. 59: Excerpts from the Index Guide and the Chemical Substance
         Index to the 9th collective period

The substance name used in the tenth and eleventh collective periods was also valid for the ninth collective period (Fig. 59).

8th COLL.   INDEX GUIDE

Piceol
   See   *Acetophenone, 4' – hydroxy – [99 – 93 – 4]*

8th COLL.   1967 – 71 – SUBJECT INDEX

Acetophenone

—, **4'–hydroxy**– [*99 – 93 – 4*], **68:** P 95514m
   aldose epimerase inhibition by, kinetics of, **73:**
      31890b
   amino acid decarboxylation in presence of, **68:**
      69304y
   antioxidants, activity of, **75:** 118877t
   ascorbic acid oxidn. by *o* –diphenol oxidase in
      presence of, **68:** 102081y
   benzoylation of, **74:** 41735q
   bond order and ir spectrum of, **75:** 135166c
   catalysts from diethylzinc and, for polymn. of
      propylene oxide, **66:** 2809g
   chromatog. of, **67:** 17608k; **69:** 56847y; **70:** 74078y
   chromophores, as model compd. for lignin, **72:**
      101961f
   coupling of, with diazotized sulfanilic acid, kinetics
      of, **74:** 127512b
   coupling reaction of, with benzenediazonium salts,
      72: 54566u
   crystal structure of, **74:** 46731v
   of *Cynanchum vincetoxicum*, **74:** 34567h
   dehydration by, of silica, **74:** P 6154c

Fig. 60: Excerpt from the Index Guide and Subject Index to the 8th
       collective period

In the Index Guide to the eighth collective period a different name can be found for the first time: 4'-hydroxy-acetophenone, once again supplemented by the CAS Registry Number (Fig. 60). Between the eighth and ninth collective periods, i.e. after 1971, many semi-systematic substance names, which had formerly been used in Chemical Abstracts, were replaced by systematic names. These systematic names provide a more precise description of the molecular structure. One advantage of this nomenclature revision was that related substances could be grouped together in the indexes due to the similarity of their systematic names. Only one Subject Index was issued for the eighth collective period and the years previously; no distinction is made between a Chemical Substance Index and a General Subject Index.

7th COLLECTIVE
SUBJECT INDEX
(1962 - 1966)

——, 1,2,3,4,5,6,6a,6b,7,8,8a,9,10,13,13a,13b,-
14,15bβ-octadecahydro-2,2,6aα,6bβ,9,-
9,13aβ-heptamethyl-10-phenyl-
methyl ester, **61**:16104e
Piceol. See *Acetophenone, 4'-hydroxy-*
Piceoside. See *Picein*
Picfume. See *Methane, trichloronitro-*
Pichia
alc. fermentation of amino acids by, **58**:
9593f; **59**:6949a
cultivation on sulfite liquor, **59**:5731d

Acetophenone (*methyl phenyl ketone*)

——, 4'-hydroxy-, **57**:3341e, 7252c; **63**:11413h
acetate, **56**:10022e
as bait for male melon fly, **61**:11268h

spectrum of, **57**:11975h; **58**:4055e; **59**:14590e;
61:7844d; **62**:9947g
benzene in relation to, **62**:8526f
electronic transitions in, **59**:14748de
in H$_2$SO$_4$, ionization and, **59**:14733h
spectrum (Raman) of, line intensities of
carbonyl group in, scattering coeffs. for,
59:2303b
textile (cellulosic) stabilization against degradation and discoloration by, **57**:8758g
textile rot proofing by, **63**:2331c
thiocarbamate, **62**:5221f; **63**:2923a; **65**:P
2171d
thiosemicarbazone, bactericidal and fungicid-
al activity of, **64**:20256e
titration of, **64**:14025f
toxicity of *p*-acetophenetidide *vs*., **58**:7284g
vibrational stretching frequency of carbonyl
group in, **60**:10519f

Fig. 61: Excerpt from the Subject Index to the 7th collective period

During the seventh collective period the Index Guide was not as yet available (it was first issued in 1967). Cross-references, subject terms and substance names are all included in the Subject Index itself (Fig. 61). Thus, a cross-reference under piceol refers to the name acetophenone, 4'-hydroxy-. In parenthesis beside acetophenone there is an additional synonym which was commonly used at that time. The structural formula with appropriately numbered positions facilitates the classification of substituents.

5th COLLECTIVE SUBJECT INDEX (1947 - 1956)

Acetophenone (*methyl phenyl ketone*),

CH₃CO—⟨hexagon⟩

——, 2'(3' and 4')-hydroxy-, azines, spectra of, 41:648b.
p-carboxyphenylhydrazones†, 43:5764g.
densities of, 45:7961i.
detn. of, 50:13663h.
isonicotinoylhydrazone†, 48:13789a.
spectra of, 50:12649g.
spectra of, and acetates, 44:10506i.
spectrum and mol.-field mechanism in, 43:2863i.
surface tension of, 49:15324i.
in Willgerodt reaction, 41:737i, 1638e.
——, 2'(and 4')-hydroxy-, 44:1929f; 45:3819f; 48:12055h; 49:4568h; 50:1661b.
acetates, hydrolysis of, 41:2707a.
as antioxidants for carotene, 45:3439d.
bactericidal action of, 43:5446e.

•

•

•

——, 4'-hydroxy-, 47:12285c; 49:1631i, 8182g; 50:874f, 11115b.
acetate, 41:738a, 43: P 3461f.
and acetate, 50:319b.
    spectroscopic study of carbonyl stretching frequency in, 48:9197b.
    spectrum of CO group in, 46:8966b.
acetate, reaction with peroxybenzoic acid, 46:7537d.
antagonism to p-aminobenzoic acid, 44:4202d.
as antioxidant for carotene, 45:3439d.

6th COLLECTIVE SUBJECT INDEX (1957 - 1961)

Acetophenone (*methyl phenyl ketone*),

CH₃CO—⟨hexagon⟩

——, 2'(and 4')-hydroxy-, 51:2664i, 6547g, 8671f, 14609c; 52:6224d, 17718i; 54:1511b, 7611e
acetates, 51:10469c**
chromatography of, 53:14041h
detection of, indophenol in, 55:12771i
and (2,4-dinitrophenyl)hydrazones, 52:13671g
effect on photographic sensitivity of carbocyanine dyes, 53:107d

•

——, 4'-hydroxy-, 51:15448c; 54:20941c
acetate, CO group absorption frequency of, 54:23799e
from Apocynum venetum, 55:3649d
chloroacetate, pesticide, 54: P 14566d
chrysanthemummonocarboxylate, insecticidal action of, 51:7639e
detn. of, 52:20896a
dimethylthiocarbamate, 55:18644h
(2,4-dinitrophenyl)hydrazone, spectrum of, 54:17232c
diphenyl arsenate, insecticide, 54: P 9196g
formation from hinokiflavone, 54:17387b, 24698d

Fig. 62: Excerpts from the Subject Indexes to the 6th and 5th collective periods

The arrangement of the Subject Index for the sixth collective period (Fig. 62) and those preceding it differs from the present form. For a substance in which the substituent can occupy different positions on a ring, the publications first listed are those which report the largest number of differently substituted compounds, e.g. 2'- and 4'-hydroxy-acetophenone or, in the Fifth Collective Index, 2'-, 3'- and 4'-hy-droxy-acetophenone. The abstract numbers referring to original publications in which only one of the possible substituted compounds is mentioned are listed last.

This combining of entries saved a lot of space. However, from the seventh collective period on, in order to improve readability of the indexes, the Chemical Abstracts Service has listed the abstract numbers of publications which report on more than one substituted compound under the name of each reported isomer separately. Consequently, a publication which mentions three isomers will be cited three times.

4th COLLECTIVE

SUBJECT INDEX

(1937 - 1946)

Acetophenone (*methyl phenyl ketone*),

——, *m*(*o* and *p*)-hydroxy-, heats of combustion and Raman spectra of, **32**: 4845⁹, 4846².⁴.⁶.

polarographic reduction potentials of, **37**: 1408⁵.

reaction of iodine, pyridine and, **40**: 1473⁵.

——, *m*(and *p*)-hydroxy-, strength exponents of, **33**: 6266².

——, *o*-hydroxy-, bromination (photochem.) of, **35**: 3527⁵.

chromium complex, **33**: 6264².

derivs., pinacols from, **31**: 4311⁶.

elec. moment of, **39**: 5142³.

esters with 1- and 2-naphthoic acids, **37**: 2374⁶.

europium deriv., fluorescence of, **36**: 3099⁵.

identification of, **37**: 130⁹.

o-methoxybenzoate, **34**: 7872².

m-nitrobenzoate, **37**: 2358⁷.

reduction potential of, **38**: 1230⁷.

and semicarbazone, **34**: 743¹.

spectrum of, **34**: 5755².

——, *o*(and *p*)-hydroxy-, **33**: 6234².

azine and hydrazone, **40**: 5012¹.

degradation of, **35**: 2874¹.

oximes, *N*-methyl derivs., **33**: 6271⁵.

•

•

•

——, *p*-hydroxy-, **33**: 6813⁹; **34**: 2814³.

acetate, **40**: 6434².

→ bactericidal action of, **40**: 2189³.

formation from picein, **39**: 4057³.

hydrogenation of, **38**: 958².

Raman spectrum of, **33**: 8117¹

reduction of, **37**: 14077⁷.

salicylate, **40**: P 2851³.

3rd COLLECTIVE

SUBJECT INDEX

(1927 - 1936)

——, *p*-hydroxy-, **21**: 3609⁵; **28**: P 4744⁴.

and derivs., **30**: 6349⁴.

methoxyacetate, **28**: 3053⁹.

2nd COLLECTIVE

SUBJECT INDEX

(1917 - 1926)

——, *p*-hydroxy-, tetraacetyl glucoside, condensation with aromatic aldehydes, **20**: 593¹.

1st COLLECTIVE

SUBJECT INDEX

(1907 - 1916)

——, *p*-hydroxy-, glucoside of, and its tetraacetyl deriv., **7**: 772⁹.

nitration of, **7**: 2933¹.

oxime, **4**: 1031⁸.

Fig. 63: Excerpt from the Subject Indexes to the 4th, 3rd, 2nd and 1st collective periods

If a retrospective literature search is to be carried out to the beginning of Chemical Abstracts, the searcher must be somewhat familiar
with the nomenclature rules and substance names used at that time, as
there was no Index Guide and no internal cross-references before 1946.
Up to the fourth collective period (1946) the substitution positions
were designated by letters (ortho-, para-, meta-positions) (Fig. 63)
rather than numbers. In addition, the abstract numbers were written in
a different form at that time, e.g. the reference to Vol. 40:2189[3] in
the Fourth Collective Index.

CHEMICAL ABSTRACTS Volume 40 (1946)

1946   **2189**   *11C—Microbiology*   **2190**

ate, a fraction I, $C_{7.26}H_{11.4}O_4$ (5.4 g.), b_{2-3} 129–134° [1] $[\alpha]_{D}^{29} = -29°$; and fraction II (6.58 g.), b_{2-3} 151–4°. Fraction I treated with $PhCH_2NH_2$ in CH_3OH, 2 hrs. at 60°, gave a dibenzylamide (III), $C_{18}H_{22}O_4N_2$, m. 103–4°, $[\alpha]_{D}^{23} = -42°$ (in 95% EtOH). III was also obtained from fraction II, and proved to be the dibenzylamide of itatartaric acid $HOOCC(OH)(CH_2OH)CH_2COOH$ (IV) by oxidation with periodic acid to a compd. $C_{18}H_{18}N_2O_2$ (V), m. 172–3°, and HCHO, followed by reduction of V with NaHg to the dibenzylamide of *dl*-malic acid. I is [2] the di-Me ester of IV; II is the lactone mono-Me ester ($CH_2O = 21.0\%$); IV has not been previously reported from a microörganism, but has been synthesized from itaconic acid. V has the structure $PhCH_2NHCOCOCH_2$- CONHCH$_2$Ph.   R. Winston Liggett

Antibacterial activity of simple derivatives of 2-amino-phenol. Mary Barber and G. A. D. Haslewood (Brit. Postgraduate Med. School, London). *Biochem. J.* **39**, [3] 285–7(1945); cf. *C.A.* **39**, 4717³.—The compds. prepd. and examd. for antibacterial activity were the following: 4 - hydroxyacetophenone, -propiophenone, -butyrophenone, and -isobutyrophenone. 4-Isobutylphenol (crystals m. 51–2°) was prepd. from 4-hydroxyisobutyrophenone; 2-amino-4-isobutylphenol was prepd. by nitration (m. 158–9° (decompn.)). 2-Amino-4-*sec*-butylphenol, m. 127–8° (decompn.) was prepd. from 4-*sec*-butylphenol. 3-Amino-4-hydroxyacetophenone, m. about 100°; 3-amino- [4] 4-hydroxypropiophenone, m. 144–5° (decompn.), 3-amino-4-hydroxybutyrophenone, m. 115–16° (decompn.). (4-Hydroxyphenyl)methylethylcarbinol, m. 120–1°, gave (4-benzoyloxyphenyl)methylethylcarbinol, m. 83–4°. A product was prepd. from the latter which is probably 4-benzoyloxy-α-ethylstyrene, m. 111–12°, from which 4-*sec*-butylphenol, m. 51–3° was made. Nuclear substitution of 2-aminophenol does not increase, and may even decrease, antibacterial activity.   S. Morgulis [5]

The effect of certain chemicals on penicillin production and mold metabolism in shake-flask fermentation. H. Koffler, S. G. Knight, R. L. Emerson, and R. H. Burris (Univ. Wisconsin, Madison). *J. Bact.* **50**, 549–59(1945). —Of 49 compds. and mixts. tested for their ability to increase penicillin shake-flask fermentation, only citric or boric acid proved to be stimulatory. The degree of

Toxicity and antibiotic activity of kojic acid by Aspergillus luteo-virescens. Harry E. Morton, Walter Kocholaty, Renate Junowicz-Kocholaty, and Albert Kelner (Univ. Pennsylvania, Philadelphia). *J. Bact.* **50**, 579–84(1945).—Kojic acid was isolated from a culture of *Aspergillus luteo-virescens*. The MLD 100 of kojic acid for 17-g. mice injected intraperitoneally was about 30 mg. The inhibitory concn. of kojic acid when dissolved in nutrient agar was tested against 166 strains of bacteria. It caused complete inhibition in a concn. of 1:500 with *Aerobacter aerogenes, Alcaligenes faecalis, Bacillus anthracis, B. megatherium, B. mesentericus, B. mycoides, B. novus, B. subtilis, Chromobacterium indicum, Clostridium novyi, Cl. putrificum, Cl. xerosis, Pneumococcus* types 2, 3, 5, 32, and 14, *Eberthella typhosa, Klebsiella pneumoniae, Pasteurella caviae, P. oviseptica, Proteus mirabilis, P. vulgaris, Pseudomonas aeruginosa, Salmonella cholerae uis, S. paratyphi, S. schottmülleri, Shigella paradysenteriae, Staphylococcus albus,* and *Streptococcus* α and β. The following were inhibited by a concn. of 1:100: *Cl. botulinum, Pneumococcus* type 1, *S. aertrycke*, and *S. pullorum.* The following were inhibited by 1:2000, *Brucella melitensis* "R," *Neisseria catarrhalis,* and *Vibrio comma. Br. suis, Pasteurella pestis,* and *Vibrio proteus* were inhibited by a concn. of 1:4000. *Leptospira icterohemorrhagiae* was inhibited by 1:100,000, and *L. canicola* by 1:1,000,000.   John T. Myers

The inhibition of sulfate-reducing bacteria by dyes. II. Practical applications in cable-storage tanks and gas holders. T. Howard Rogers and E. C. Barton-Wright (Brit. Nonferrous Metals Assoc.). *J. Soc. Chem. Ind.* **64**, 292–5(1945); cf. *C.A.* **34**, 4100⁵.—The use of flavine dyes has been applied to the prevention of H_2S corrosion on cables stored under water. Except with very dense growth a dye concn. of 1:250,000 was effective both in storage tanks and in the cable works. Similar treatment of the sealing water for gas holders gave promising results.   E. R. Newton

Method for the rapid production of citrinin. J. Wyllie (Queen's Univ., Kingston, Ont.). *Can. J. Pub. Health* **36**, 477–83(1945).—A yield of 4.5 g. of citrinin per 1. can be obtained in 10 days, or 5.5 g. per 1. in 15 days, by cultivating Timonin's strain (*C.A.* 28, 2994⁷) of *Aspergillus*

Fig. 64: Abstracts from Vol. 40

Fig. 64 shows an excerpt from the Vol. 40 Chemical Abstracts issue. Here the columns are numbered rather than the individual abstracts. The length of the column is numerically subdivided from 1 to 9. In the index these numbers are written in superscript. They do not denote the beginning of an abstract, but rather the section of the page in which the substance is mentioned. As these numbers do not identify individual abstracts, they were called CA accession numbers, not abstract numbers prior to 1967.

3 Locating the Source Document

3.1 CAS Source Index (CASSI)

The abstract texts in Chemical Abstracts are not intended as substitutes for the contents of the original document. They should, however, furnish the reader with enough information to enable him to decide whether intensive study of the original document is worthwhile. The CAS Source Index provides the link between the CA abstract and the original literature. CASSI not only includes every type of publication, such as journals, technical reports, monographs, conference reports and patent groups, which have been cited in Chemical Abstracts from 1907 to the present time, but also all source material cited in Beilsteins Handbuch der Organischen Chemie up to and including 1963 and in Chemisches Zentralblatt from 1830 to 1940. Libraries in 28 countries, which hold the cited journal or book, are named beside the publication source entry.

In the introduction to CASSI there is a directory of all publishers and sales organizations whose publications are cited in Chemical Abstracts. This "Dictionary of Publishers and Sales Agencies" gives the full name and address beside each name code (Fig. 66) so that books, conference proceedings, journals and other documents can be directly ordered from the publishers.

CAS SOURCE INDEX   1907-1984 CUMULATIVE

DIRECTORY OF PUBLISHERS AND

SALES AGENCIES

AAAS	American Association for the Advancement of Science 1515 Massachusetts Ave., N.W. Washington, DC USA 20005
AAEC	Australian Atomic Energy Commission Research Establishment Library, Private Mail Bag Sutherland, N. S. W. 2232, Australia
AAPG	American Association of Petroleum Geologists POB 979 Tulsa, OK USA 74101
Valgus	Izdatel'stvo Valgus Tallinn, USSR
Valt Tek Tutkimuskeskus	Valtion Teknillinen Tutkimuskeskus Vuorimiehentie 5 SF–02150 Espoo 15, Finland
Vandenhoeck & Ruprecht	Vandenhoeck & Ruprecht Postfach 77 D–3400 Goettingen, Fed. Rep. Ger.
Van Nostrand Reinhold	Van Nostrand Reinhold 135 W. 50th St. New York, NY USA 10020
VCH (Deerfield Beach)	VCH Publishers, Inc. 303 N.W. 12th Ave. Deerfield Beach, FL USA 33441
VCH (Weinheim)	VCH Verlagsgesellschaft mbH Postfach 1260/1280 D–6940 Weinheim, Fed. Rep. Ger
VDE–Verlag	VDE–Verlag Bismarckstrasse 33 D–1000 Berlin 12, Fed. Rep. Ger.
VDI–Verlag	VDI–Verlag GmbH Postfach 1139 D–4000 Duesseldorf 1, Fed. Rep. Ger.

Fig. 65: Excerpt from the directory of publishers and sales organizations in the CAS Source Index

CAS SOURCE INDEX   1907–1984 CUMULATIVE

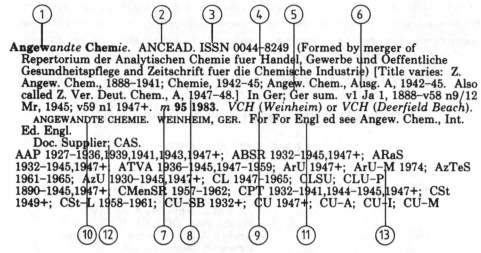

Ange*wandte* **Chem***ie.* ANCEAD. ISSN 0044–8249 (Formed by merger of
Repertorium der Analytischen Chemie fuer Handel, Gewerbe und Oeffentliche
Gesundheitspflege and Zeitschrift fuer die Chemische Industrie) [Title varies: Z.
Angew. Chem., 1888–1941; Chemie, 1942–45; Angew. Chem., Ausg. A, 1942–45. Also
called Z. Ver. Deut. Chem., A, 1947–48.] In Ger; Ger sum. v1 Ja 1, 1888–v58 n9/12
Mr, 1945; v59 n1 1947+. *m* **95** **1983.** *VCH (Weinheim)* or *VCH (Deerfield Beach).*
    ANGEWANDTE CHEMIE. WEINHEIM, GER. For For Engl ed see Angew. Chem., Int.
Ed. Engl.
    Doc. Supplier: CAS.
AAP 1927–1936,1939,1941,1943,1947+; ABSR 1932–1945,1947+; ARaS
1932–1945,1947+ ATVA 1936–1945,1947–1959; ArU 1947+; ArU–M 1974; AzTeS
1961–1965; AzU 1930–1945,1947+; CL 1947–1965; CLSU; CLU–P
1890–1945,1947+ CMenSR 1957–1962; CPT 1932–1941,1944–1945,1947+; CSt
1949+; CSt–L 1958–1961; CU–SB 1932+; CU 1947+; CU–A; CU–I; CU–M

UkLC 1932–1945,1947+; Uk 1932+; UkLS 1932–1945,1947+; UkShU 1958–1962;
GuGIC 1959–1964; GyDaD 1950+; GyDaM 1888–1950,1951*,1952,1953*,1954+;
GyHTIB; GyJuK 1923–1945,1947+; GyKG 1932+; GyMB; GyWK; HuBM
1932–1941,1949+; IiNI 1941–1944,1958+; IeDL 1963–1964,1966–1968; IsRW
1932–1945,1947+; ItRC 1931–1962,1967–1968; JOU; JTJ 1958+; JTNDL; MxMC
1951–1966; NeDTH 1932+; NeHB 1932–1941,1949+; NoTU–T; RuLA
1888–1914,1924,1927–1945,1947+; RuMG 1932–1945,1947+; SaPS 1947–1964;
SpBaU–SQ 1932–1941,1942*–1943*,1947–1977; SwSK 1947+; SzGE 1892–1970;
SzZE 1947+

Ange*wandte* **Chem***ie,* **Ausg***abe* **A:** *Wissenschaftlicher Teil.* See **Angew. Chem.**

Ange*wandte* **Chem***ie,* **Ausg***abe* **B:** *Technisch–Wirtschaftlicher–Teil.* See
Chem.–Ing.–Tech.

Ange*wandte* **Chem***ie,* **Beil***age.* See **Nachr. Chem. Tech.**

Ange*wandte* **Chem***ie,* **International Edition in English.** ACIEAY. ISSN 0570–0833.
In Eng; Eng sum. v1 n1 Ja, 1962+. [Pub a preliminary issue (n0) in My, 1961.] *m*
23 1984. *VCH (Weinheim)* or *VCH (Deerfield Beach).*
    ANGEWANDTE CHEMIE. INTERNATIONAL EDITION IN ENGLISH. WEINHEIM, GER. For
Ger ed see Angew. Chem.
ABSR; ARaS; ATVA; AU–M 1962–1973; AkU 1962; ArU; ArU–M; AzTeS;
AzU; C; CL; CLSU; CLSU–M; CLU–P; CLU–M; CMenSR 1976–1979; CPT;
CSf; CSt; CU–SB; CU; CU–A; CU–I; CU–M; CU–Riv; CU–RivP; CU–S;
CU–SC; CoU; CoU–M; CtU; CtW; CtY–M; DBS; DGU; DLC; DNAL; DNLM;
DP; DeU; DeWDJ; DeWDL; DeWH; FMU; FTaSU; FU; GAT; GEU; GU;

Fig. 66: Excerpt from the CAS Source Index

Fig. 66 shows that the former titles of "Angewandte Chemie" have cross-references to the newly created journals listed under their abbreviated titles.

Explanation of Fig. 66:

1. Title of the journal or publication source in abbreviated form. The journal titles are arranged in alphabetic order of the title abbreviations printed in boldface type. The titles are abbreviated according to the rules of the International Standards Organization (ISO) and are, of course, consistently used in Chemical Abstracts as well as in the bibliographic data of all the other CAS services.
2. ASTM CODEN, an unambiguous and computer-readable code for the titles of scientific and technical journals and other non-periodical publications.
3. ISSN (International Standard Serial Number) or ISBN (International Standard Book Number)
4. Former title and title changes (possible translation of the title if it is written in a language other than English, German, French, Spanish or Latin)
5. Language of publication and language of the summary
6. History of the publication (Volume 1 appeared on January 1st 1888, Number 9/12 was issued in March 1945; after a suspension of publication the first issue of Volume 59 appeared in 1947. The plus sign after 1947 indicates that publication of the journal has continued without interruption up to the present day.)
7. Frequency of publication (monthly)
8. Number and year of the volume last entered into the CAS database
9. Publisher's name
10. Title written according to the American Library Association's Anglo-American cataloguing rules (ALA/AACR)
11. Reference to additional editions of the journal or to a change in title
12. Document supplier code indicating other abstracting or indexing organizations which cover that publication in their secondary services
13. Coded names of the libraries which hold the journal; first the American libraries, then the libraries of the remaining countries in alphabetical order of their codes

References to libraries are given in a code which contains the following information:

1. Abbreviated symbols for the country (or, for U.S. libraries, the state) and the library
2. Inclusive years of library holdings of the publication (the plus sign denotes continuous holding of the journal from that date onwards, an asterisk beside a given year indicates that not all the issues for that year are present).

A directory containing the complete address of each participating
library is found in the introduction to CASSI (Fig. 67). These libraries have declared their willingness to make the appropriate literature
available on request.

CAS SOURCE INDEX   1907–1984 CUMULATIVE

AVAILABILITY OF LISTED PUBLICATIONS

DIRECTORY OF PARTICIPATING LIBRARIES

UNITED STATES OF AMERICA

Alabama

AAP	Ralph Brown Draughon Library Auburn University Auburn, AL 36849
AB	Birmingham Public and Jefferson County Free Library Technology Department 2020 Seventh Avenue, North Birmingham, AL 35203
ABSR	Southern Research Institute Library POB 55305 Birmingham, AL 35255–5305

United Kingdom

Uk	British Library Science References Library Holborn Division 25 Southampton Buildings Chancery Lane London WC2A 1AW Engl. Bayswater Division 10 Porchester Garden London W2 4DE Engl.
UkHA	Atomic Energy Research Establishment Library Harwell, Didcot, Oxon. OX11 0RB Engl.
UkLC	Royal Society of Chemistry Library Burlington House London W1V 0BN Engl.

Fig. 67: Excerpt from the directory of libraries in the CAS Source
       Index

CASSI is published in updated form every five years. A quarterly supplement is issued containing information about journal title changes, new journals or changes in library holdings. Besides new entries, the fourth quarterly supplement of each year includes the cumulated data contained in the three preceding issues. Moreover, it lists the 1000 journals most frequently cited in Chemical Abstracts
- alphabetically arranged according to their abbreviated titles
- arranged according to the frequency of their citation
The next cumulative edition of the CAS Source Index is due to be published in 1990.

89: 162686t **Kinetics of the reaction of cyclohexene with thiocyanogen.** Kartashov, V. R.; Akimkina, N. F.; Skorobogatova, E. V.; Sanina, N. L. (Gor'k. Politekh. Inst., Gorkiy, USSR). *Kinet. Katal.* **1978,** 19(3), 785-8 (Russ). Kinetic data for the

reaction of cyclohexene with $(SCN)_2$ in HOAc suggested a relatively polar cyclic transition state. The products were **I** (R = SCN, NCS, OAc).

Fig. 68: Abstract from CA Vol. 89

Kinet*ika i* **Katal***iz.* KNKTA4 (Kinetics and Catalysis). In Russ; Russ sum; Eng tc. vl nl My/Je, 1960+. *bm* 14 1973. *USSR* [*Sub*].
KINETIKA I KATALIZ. MOSCOW. For Engl transl see Kinet. Catal. (Engl. Transl.).

Sec Serv: CAS, ISI
CLU 1963+; CU; CU-S 1961+; DBS 1964+; DLC; FMU; GAT 1961-1964; ICRL; IU 1960-1961,1967+; LU; MCM; MH-C 1964-1972; MiU; MoKL; NIC; NN 1963+; NNC 1961+; NRU; NjP; OCoB; PPF; RPB 1961+; TxBeaL 1963+; ViU 1960*,1961-1964,1965*-1966*; WaU; AgBU-C 1961-1964; BeBB 1967+; CaBVaU; CaOOM 1962; CaOON 1961+; CzPS; FrPU 1961+; FrPU-OS; GbHA 1963+; GbLC; GbLN; GbSU; GyDD 1961+; GyJK; HuBM; IiNI; IsRW; ItRC 1964+; JpTJ 1962+; JpTN; RuLA; RuMG 1961+; SvSK; SzZE 1964+

Fig. 69: Excerpt from the CAS Source Index

Kinet*ics and* **Catal***ysis* (**Engl***ish* **Translat***ion*). KICAA8 (Transl of Kinet. Katal.). In Eng; Eng sum. vl nl My/Je, 1960+. *bm* **1973.** *Plenum (New York).*
KINETICS AND CATALYSIS. NEW YORK. (ENGLISH TRANSLATION OF KINETIKA I KATALIZ)
Sec Serv: CAS
CLSU; CLU; CMenSR 1961+; CPT 1965+; CSt; CU SB; CU; CU-S; CoFS 1970+; CoU; CtU 1963+; CtW 1964+; DBS 1963+; DLC; DNAL 1967+; DeU 1969+; DeWDJ 1962+; DeWDL; DeWH; GAT; GU 1969+; IArg; ICJ; IEN; IU 1968+; IaAS; IaU; InLP; InU; KU; KyLoU 1965+; MCM; MH-C 1973+; MdU; MdU-C; MiDW 1967+; MiKUp 1966+; MiMidD; MnU; MoSW 1963+; MoU; N; NAlU 1961+; NAlfC 1967+; NBPol; NBuA; NBuU; NIC; NNE 1964+; NObSU; NRU; NSyU; NUpB 1965+; NbU 1970+; NcD 1964+; NcRS; NcU; NjP 1962+; NjRahM 1963+; OAkU 1964+; OClCS; OCoB; OTU 1966+; OU; OkS; OrCS 1967+; OrU 1966+; PBL; PPD 1965+; PPF 1962+; PPi 1967+; PPiM 1963+; PPiU; PPiUSM 1960-1964; PSt; TxBeaL; TxCM 1964+; TxDW; TxHR 1968+; TxLT; TxU 1965+; ViBlbV 1964+; ViRVI 1961-1962,1964+; WU 1965+; WU-E; WaPS; WaU; WyU 1964+; AuMU 1963+; BeBB; CaBVaU; CaNSHD; CaOKQ; CaOLU 1964+; CaOOM; CaOON; CaQMM; GbLC; GbLN; GyJK; <u>JpTN;</u> NoTN

Fig. 70: Excerpt from the CAS Source Index

3.2 Sample search: Where can the English translation of the document
                   covered in CA abstract No. 89:162686t be obtained?
   To illustrate: Short journal titles
                  CAS Source Index
                  Library holdings information
                  English translations

The original paper covered in Chemical Abstracts Vol. 89 under the abstract number 162696t (Fig. 68) appeared in the journal with the abbreviated title of "Kinet. Katal."

From the CAS Source Index it is possible to discover that the complete
title of the journal is: Kinetika i Kataliz (Fig. 69). It is published
in the Russian language and the summary is also in Russian. It includes, however, a table of contents (tc) in English. An English
translation of "Kinetika i Kataliz" is also issued and a reference to
the short journal title, Kinet. Catal. (Engl. Transl.), is given in
CASSI.

The complete title of the English translation is found in the alphabetical list of short titles: Kinetics and Catalysts (English Translation) (Fig. 70).

This journal is held by one Japanese library, the National Diet Library in Tokyo (JpTN). No year designation following the library code
signifies that it holds a complete set of the journal.

4 Registry Handbooks

4.1 Registry Handbook - Number Section

The Registry Handbook - Number Section contains all the CAS Registry Numbers so far assigned. It is, therefore, a part of the CAS Registry database which was described on p. 4.

Consecutive Registry Numbers are awarded to each new substance registered in the CAS database. Although they contain no inherent information about the chemical composition or structure of the substance, they represent a unique identification tag for each substance and its stereochemical descriptor. These CAS Registry Numbers have grown increasingly important in recent years not only because they are cited in many journals, but also because chemical manufacturers are required to use them in accordance with the new laws governing chemicals. Furthermore, the Registry Number is especially important and helpful for online searches in the databases of the Chemical Abstracts Service, but the CAS Registry Numbers are also used in many other chemical databases offered for online searches. By quoting the CAS Registry Number listing of all possible alternative substance names becomes unnecessary, thus eliminating possible sources of error. It is, therefore, imperative that the CAS Registry Number itself is correct. This can be verified by the last digit which is a check number calculated from the preceding numbers using the following formula:

$$\frac{iN_i + \ldots + 4N_4 + 3N_3 + 2N_2 + 1N_1}{10} = \text{whole number} + \frac{5}{10}$$

N: The digits of the CAS Registry Number from right to left, excluding the check number
R: Check number
Example: 7732-18-5

$$\frac{6x7 + 5x7 + 4x3 + 3x2 + 2x1 + 1x8}{10} = 10 + \frac{5}{10}$$

The systematic CA Index Name belonging to each Registry Number is given in the Registry Handbook - Number Section. Each year three supplements to the Registry Handbook - Number Section are issued listing approximately 560,000 new substances which are registered in the Registry database each year. The structure of about 3 % of the substances

newly cited in the chemical literature has not yet been fully resolved. But these substances are also awarded a CAS Registry Number.
After definitive identification of the structure, some prove to be
previously known and registered substances. As one single substance
now has two CAS Registry Numbers, the number which is least used in
the literature and documentation is deleted. These changes of CAS Registry Numbers for a substance are announced in the supplement "Registry Handbook - Registry Number Update". A cumulative issue of this
supplement is published annually. When a literature search is carried
out using CAS Registry Numbers the latest issue of the Registry Number
Update should be consulted to determine if it contains a cross-reference to another Registry Number. If two numbers do exist for one substance, both should be used in a computer search to ensure that all
literature is located.

Structural analysis sometimes reveals a mixture of different substances which were originally registered as one substance. In this
case the CAS Registry Number is also unjustified and must be completely deleted. In the Registry Number Update the number is followed by
the note: No longer in use.

It is possible that searches using the CAS Registry Numbers or the
appropriate substance names reveal no abstract in Chemical Abstracts
or in the CA database. Not all substances stored in the CAS database
are mentioned in Chemical Abstracts. The Chemical Abstracts Service
cooperates with other organizations and companies which have chemical
substances registered in the CAS Registry System, although these substances have not yet been published and therefore, cannot have appeared in Chemical Abstracts. Parent compounds are also awarded CAS
Registry Numbers even though they are not themselves described in the
literature, but only their substituted derivatives. The Chemical Abstracts Service stores and registers the parent compounds in order to
establish the systematic substance names and to facilitate the future
designation of new substances.

4.2 Registry Handbook - Common Names

The Registry Handbook - Common Names is a convenient tool for quickly
solving nomenclature problems and for evolving search strategies for
online searches. It is part of the CAS Registry File. In addition to

the CAS Registry Numbers and the systematic CA Index Names, the semi-systematic names used by authors in their publications, trade and trivial names are filed. The Registry Handbook - Common Names (1986 edition) contains approximately 1,250,000 names corresponding to more than 500,000 chemical substances. The trivial names and semi-systematic names are selected by means of a precisely defined computer program. All names which are too long and complicated are excluded e.g. those bearing stereochemical information, those including three or more hyphens or those composed of more than 35 letters. The selection is based on all the 8.4 million names stored in the Registry File from 1967 to the present, but some of the names from the seventh collective period (1962 to 1966) are also included, as the Chemical Abstracts Service is in the process of adding the information from this period to the file.

The Registry Handbook - Common Names - consists of two parts:

Name Section

The "Name Section" contains about 1,250,000 substance names listed alphabetically. Each name is succeeded by the CAS Registry Number (in square brackets) and the molecular formula. The CA Index Name can be found in the "Number Section" using the CAS Registry Number.

Nicotine *[54-11-5]* $C_{10}H_{14}N_2$
(-)-Nicotine *[54-11-5]* $C_{10}H_{14}N_2$
(±)-Nicotine *[22083-74-5]* $C_{10}H_{14}N_2$
(+)-Nicotine *[25162-00-9]* $C_{10}H_{14}N_2$
Nicotine-*N'-d*$_3$ *[65636-94-4]* $C_{10}H_{11}D_3N_2$
Nicotine-2'-*d* *[65636-95-5]* $C_{10}H_{13}DN_2$
Nicotine-^{14}*C* *[16586-18-8]* $C_{10}H_{14}N_2$
d-Nicotine *[25162-00-9]* $C_{10}H_{14}N_2$
D-Nicotine *[25162-00-9]* $C_{10}H_{14}N_2$
DL-Nicotine *[22083-74-5]* $C_{10}H_{14}N_2$

Fig. 71: Excerpt from the Registry Handbook - Common Names, Name
        Section

Number Section

About 500,000 CAS Registry Numbers are listed in this part. Each CAS Registry Number is followed by the molecular formula, the systematic Index Names from the different collective periods and the various trivial names which are also included in the "Name Section".

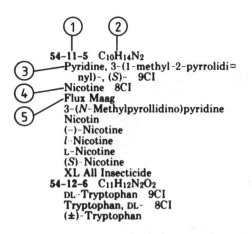

54-11-5 $C_{10}H_{14}N_2$
Pyridine, 3-(1-methyl-2-pyrrolidi=
    nyl)-, (*S*)-   9CI
Nicotine   8CI
Flux Maag
3-(*N*-Methylpyrollidino)pyridine
Nicotin
(-)-Nicotine
l-Nicotine
L-Nicotine
(*S*)-Nicotine
XL All Insecticide
54-12-6 $C_{11}H_{12}N_2O_2$
DL-Tryptophan   9CI
Tryptophan, DL-   8CI
(±)-Tryptophan

Fig. 72: Excerpt from the Registry Handbook - Common Names, Number
      Section

     1. CAS Registry Number
     2. Molecular formula
     3. The systematic CA Index Name used in the current Chemical
        Substance Index. The symbol "9CI" after the substance name
        indicates that this name is valid from the ninth collec-
        tive period (i.e. from 1972) to the present day.
     4. The systematic substance name used in the eighth collec-
        tive period.
     5. Appropriate semi-systematic, trade, and trivial names in
        alphabetical order

Not all the substances listed in the Registry Handbook - Common Names
have been mentioned in Chemical Abstracts, as the Chemical Abstracts
Service also awards CAS Registry Numbers to substances which have been
included in other publications, e.g. Colour Index, Merck Index or
other organizations like BioSiences Information Service, but which
have not been described in the primary literature.

Some CAS Registry Numbers in the Registry Handbook - Common Names are
marked with an asterisk which indicates that this number was not assigned according to the usual rules of the CAS Registry database.
Thus, a substance marked by an asterisk can be found either in the
General Subject Index, as it is the designation for an imprecisely
defined group of substances, or it is listed in the Chemical Substance
Index as an incompletely defined derivative of a known substance.

The Registry Handbook - Common Names provides a simple method of determining which chemical substance is meant by a trade or trivial name
or vice versa and which other names are known for a certain substance.
This is especially important for literature searches in which no CAS
Registry Numbers can be used, only substance names.

1972–1976 FORMULA INDEX

C25H25N3O4S
  Acetamide, N-[3-(1-acetyl-1,4-dihydro-4-☌
    pyridinyl)-1-methyl-1H-indol-2-yl]-N-☌
    [(4-methylphenyl)sulfonyl]- [*38829–47–9*], **77:**
    151799h
  Benzamide, N-[2-[4-[[[[(2-phenylcyclopropyl)☌
    amino]carbonyl]amino]sulfonyl]phenyl]☌
    ethyl]-
    trans- [*25256–55–7*], **82:** P 43073m
  Benzenesulfonamide, 4-[[1-(4-ethylbenzoyl)-2-☌
    oxopropyl]azo]-N-(2-methylphenyl)-
    [*58279–37–1*], **84:** 58831x; **85:** 46472p
  Benzenesulfonic acid, 4-methyl-
    [3,4-dihydro-6,7-dimethoxy-2-(4-☌
    pyridinylmethylene)-1(2H)-☌
    naphthalenylidene]hydrazide [*52838–06–9*], **81:**
    P 25661b
  4-Imidazolidinecarboxylic acid, 2-oxo-1,3-bis☌
    (phenylmethyl)-5-[[[1-(2-thienyl)ethyl]☌
    amino]carbonyl]- [*51591–85–6*], **80:** P 95951z
  1,2,4-Thiadiazolidin-3-one, 2-benzoyl-5-[4-☌
    (diethylamino)phenyl]-4-phenyl-
    1,1-dioxide [*56905–74–9*], **83:** 164092w
➙ **C25H25N3O4Zn**
  Zinc, bis(3-oxo-N-phenylbutanamidato-O,O')☌
    (pyridine)- [*38800–53–2*], **77:** 121585t
C25H25N3O5
  2H-Benzotriazole, 5,6-dimethoxy-2-[4-[2-(3,4,5-☌
    trimethoxyphenyl)ethenyl]phenyl]-
    (E)- [*38549–86–9*], **77:** 164607u

Fig. 73: Excerpt from the Formula Index to the 9th collective period

4.3 Sample search: Were there any publications about the following substance or any of its derivatives in the period from 1972 to 1976?

$$
\begin{array}{c}
\text{H} \\
\text{N} \\
\text{C} = \text{N} - \text{SO}_2 - \bigcirc \\
\text{C} \\
\text{H}_2\text{C} \quad \text{CH} - \text{NH} - \text{SO}_2 - \bigcirc \\
\text{H}_2\text{C} \quad \text{CH}_2 \\
\text{C} \\
\text{H}_2
\end{array}
$$

To illustrate: Formula Index
           Index of Ring Systems
           Chemical Substance Index
           Registry Handbook - Number Section

The systematic CA Index Name for this substance is unknown and it is time-consuming to derive it using the rules of nomenclature. The fastest method of solving this problem is to look up the molecular formula $C_{25}H_{25}N_3O_4S_2$ in the Ninth Collective Formula Index (1972 to 1976) (Fig. 73). As this molecular formula is not included, nothing about the substance itself was published in the years from 1972 to 1976. However, the problem also addressed its derivatives.

1972–1976 IRS

3-RING SYSTEMS

5,5,58
C_4S–C_4S–$C_{40}O_{18}$
  $1H,3H,30H,33H$–Dithieno[3,4–a_1:3',4'–d_2][1,4,7,=
   10,13,16,19,22,25,30,33,36,39,42,45,48,51,54]=
   octadecaoxacyclooctapentacontin
5,6,6
CN_4–C_3N_3–C_4N_2
  Tetrazolo[1',5':1,6]pyrimido[5,4–e][1,2,4]triazine
CN_4–C_3N_3–C_5N
  Pyrido[2,3–e]tetrazolo[5,1–c][1,2,4]triazine

•

•

•

C_4N–C_6–C_6
  14–Azadispiro[5.1.5.2]pentadecane
  Benz[cd]indole
  $1H$–Benz[e]indole
  $1H$–Benz[f]indole
  $1H$–Benz[g]indole
  $1H$–Benz[e]isoindole
  $1H$–Benz[f]isoindole
  $1H$–Carbazole
  4,7–Ethano–$1H$–isoindole
  4a,8a–(Methaniminomethano)naphthalene
  1,4–Methano–$1H$–2–benzazepine
  1,4–Methano–$1H$–3–benzazepine
  3,6–Methano–$1H$–indole
  Spiro[bicyclo[3.3.1]nonane–9,3'–pyrrolidine]
  Spiro[cyclohexane–1,3'–[3H]indole]
  Spiro[cyclohexane–1,5'–[5H]indole]
  Spiro[cyclohexane–1,1'–[1H]isoindole]
  Spiro[naphthalene–1(2H),3'–[3H]pyrrole]
  Spiro[naphthalene–2(1H),3'–[3H]pyrrole]
  Spiro[naphthalene–1(2H),3'–pyrrolidine]

Fig. 74: Excerpt from the Index of Ring Systems to the 9th collective
        period

The structure diagram shows that the substance is a benzenesulfonamide. More than 130 pages of abstracts about this class of compound
are listed in the Ninth Collective Chemical Substance Index. It is extremely time-consuming to check the individual names, not to mention
the abstracts themselves. As the original substance contains an uncommon ring system, it is possible to derive the systematic CA Index Name
by means of ring analysis. The ring analysis for this substance is:

      3-Ring System

       5,6,6

        $C_4N-C_6-C_6$

In the Index of Ring Systems for the ninth collective period there are
various substance names mentioned under this ring analysis (Fig. 74).
Every chemist should recognize that this ring system is a spiro substance. Thus, the choice of alternative names to be consulted in the
Chemical Substance Index is reduced to three.

1972–1976 CHEM. SUBSTANCE INDEX

Spiro[cyclohexane-1,3'-[3H]indole] [171-74-4]

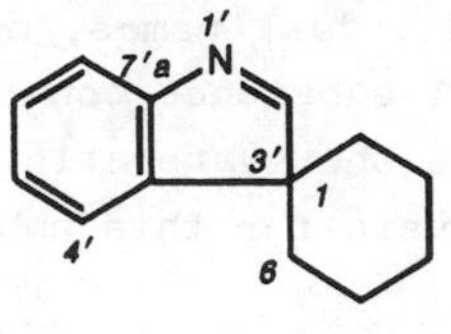

benzenesulfonamide deriv. [52850-92-7], **81:** 25490
benzenesulfonamide deriv. [59238-82-3], **84:**
       164559z
——, **2'-methyl-** [13141-50-9], **76:** 25082k
coupling of, with diazotized aniline, **82:** P 59915y
Spiro[cyclohexane-1,5'-[5H]indole] [55429-97-5]

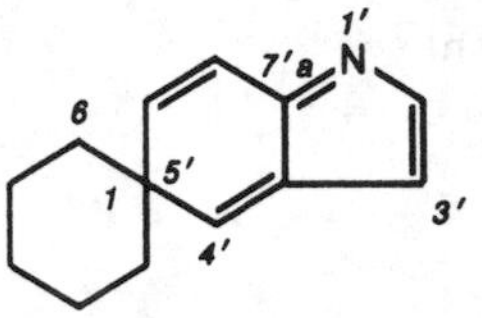

Spiro[cyclohexane-1,3'-[3H]indole]-2'-⊸
       carboxaldehyde
phenylhydrazone [53815-17-1], methylation of, **82:** P
       59915y

Fig. 75: Excerpt from the Chemical Substance Index to the 9th collec-
       tive period

Under the name "spiro-[cyclohexane-1,3'-[3H]indole]" the Chemical Substance Index shows the structure diagram immediately after the CAS Registry Number. Now it can be ascertained if this is the correct ring system (Fig. 75). The structure diagram of all cyclic parent compounds, i.e. all compounds mentioned in the Index of Ring Systems, are illustrated in the Chemical Substance Index. These ring skeletons are also shown in the Ring Systems Handbook (cf. chap. 5, p. 122).

The structure diagram is followed by two references to abstracts about benzenesulfonamide derivatives.

25490v   Reactions of p-toluenesulfonyl azide with derivatives of cyclohept- and cyclooctindole. Bailey, A. Sydney; Seager, John F. (Dyson Perrins Lab., Oxford, Engl.).   *J. Chem. Soc., Perkin Trans. 1* 1974, (7), 763–70 (Eng).   The hexahydrocyclo-

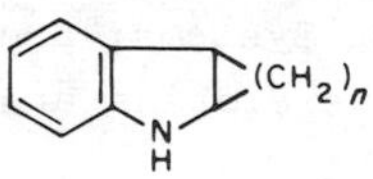

I. *n* = 5
II. *n* = 6

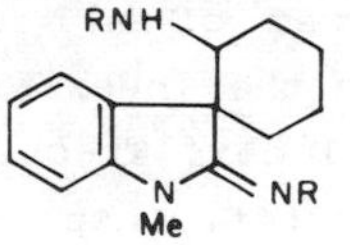

R = —SO₂——Me

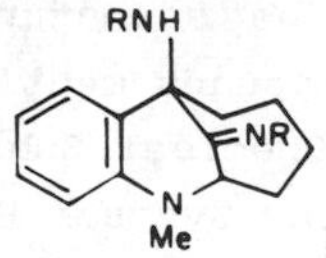

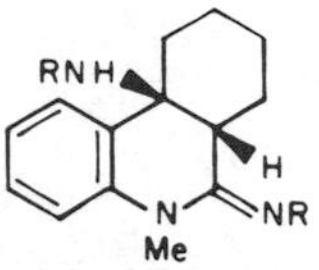

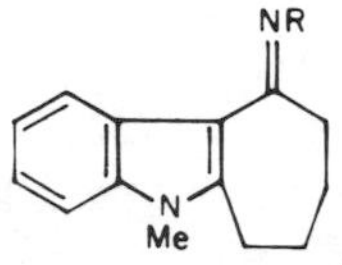

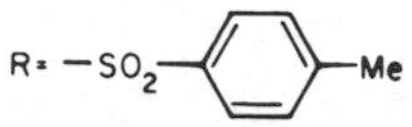

hept- and -octindoles (**I** and **II**) with 4-MeC₆H₄SO₂N₃ gave 33 and 88% of the corresponding 6,7.8,9,10,10a-hexahydro-10a- and 7,8,9,10,11,11a - hexahydro - 11a - *p* - tolylsulfonylamino derivs., resp.   The *N*-Me deriv. of **I** with 4-MeC₆H₄SO₂N₃ gave the indolespirocyclohexane (**III**), the benzazonine (**IV**), the phenanthridine (**V**), and the cycloheptindole (**VI**), resp.   The *N*-Me deriv. of **II** reacted similarly.

Fig. 76: CA abstract from Vol. 81

Although numerous additional structure diagrams are shown in the abstract itself, it is impossible to determine which is the structure being sought (Fig. 76 and 77).

84: 164559z Further examination of the reaction between hexahydro-N-methyl-cyclohept[b]indole and arenesulfonyl azides. Bailey, A. Sydney; Wilkinson, Patricia A. (Dyson Perrins Lab., Univ. Oxford, Oxford, Engl.). *J. Chem. Soc., Perkin Trans. 1* **1976**, (5), 481–4 (Eng). 5,6,7,8,9,10-Hexa⁼

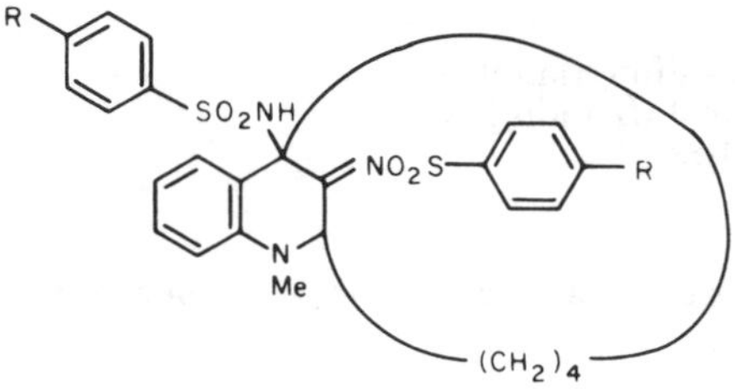

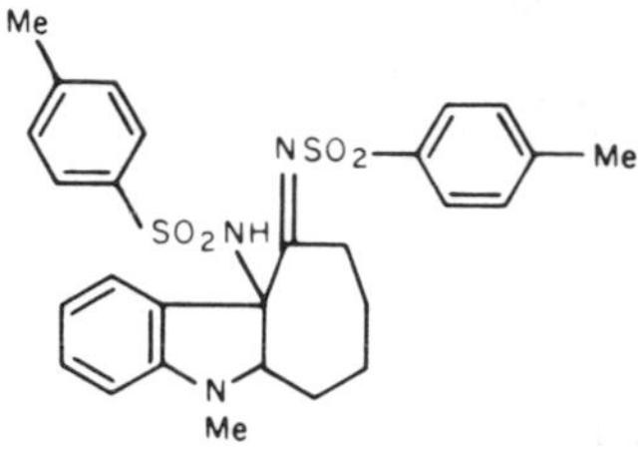

hydro-5-methylcyclohept[*b*]indole (**I**) underwent reaction with 4-MeC₆H₄SO₂N₃ in CCl₄ to give the benzazonine **II** (R = Me) and the compd. to which this structure was previously assigned (B, 1974) was reformulated as the indole **III**. **I** also underwent reaction with 4-ClC₆H₄SO₂N₃ to give **II** (R = Cl) and the eactions of this compd. were examd. and compared with those of the pyrroloquinoline **IV**.

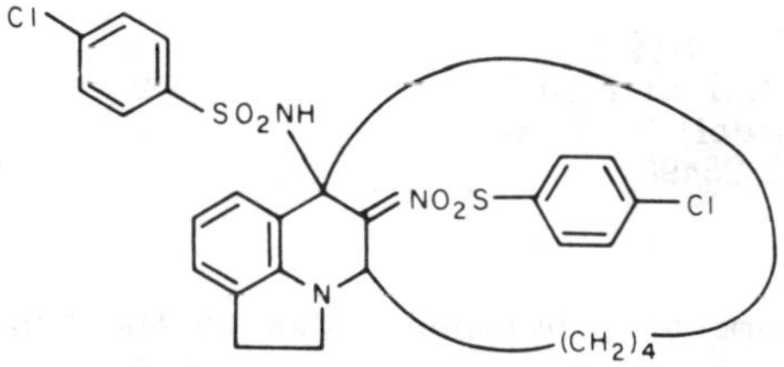

Fig. 77: CA abstract from Vol. 84

CAS REGISTRY HANDBOOK

52850-92-7   Benzenesulfonamide,
N-[1',2'-dihydro-1'-methyl-2'-[[(4-⊃
methylphenyl)sulfonyl]imino]spiro[cyclohexane-1,⊃
3'-[3H]indol]-2-yl]-4-methyl- $C_{28}H_{31}N_3O_4S_2$

•

•

•

59238-82-3   Benzenesulfonamide,
4-chloro-N-[2-[[(4-chlorophenyl)sulfonyl]amin⊃
o]-1'-methylspiro[cyclohexane-1,3'-[3H]indol]-2'⊃
(1'H)-ylidene]- $C_{26}H_{25}Cl_2N_3O_4S_2$

Fig. 78: Excerpt from the Registry Handbook - Number Section

1972-1976 CHEM. SUBSTANCE INDEX

Benzenesulfonamide,

——, **4-chloro-N-[2-[[(4-chlorophenyl)⊃
sulfonyl]amino]-1'-methylspiro⊃
[cyclohexane-1,3'-[3H]indol]-2'(1'H)-⊃
ylidene]-** [*59238-82-3*], 84: 164559z

•

•

•

——, **N-[1',2'-dihydro-1'-methyl-2'-[[(4-⊃
methylphenyl)sulfonyl]imino]spiro⊃
[cyclohexane-1,3'-[3H]indol]-2-yl]-4-⊃
methyl-** [*52850-92-7*], 81: 25490v

Fig. 79: Excerpt from the Chemical Substance Index to the 9th collective

In this case, however, an additional piece of information from the Chemical Substance Index is useful (Fig. 75): the general designation "benzenesulfonamide derivative", given here instead of the the usual systematic CA Index Name, signifies that the substance is listed under benzenesulfonamide, as was initially presumed. However, a CAS Registry Number for these derivatives is shown. The systematic CA Index Name can be determined using this number in the Registry Handbook – Number Section (Fig. 78). The names finally show what the derivatives of spiro-[cyclohexane-1,3'-[3H]indole] look like. Futhermore, the systematic CA Index Names offer the possibility of consulting the Chemical Substance Index and utilizing the text modifications to ascertain the context in which the substances were mentioned in the original documents (Fig. 79). However, as only an abstract number is given for both substances and no text modifications, this signifies that the authors reported only on the synthesis. If special purification methods, analysis data or the like had been mentioned in the publication, the Chemical Abstracts Service would have added this as a text modification.

5 Ring Systems Handbook

The Ring Systems Handbook, which replaced the Parent Compound Handbook and has been published since 1984, contains all the presently known basic structural skeletons, the parent compounds of cyclic substances, i.e. ring systems without substituents. The Handbook includes approximately 60,000 ring and cage systems. It is a complete work of reference which provides access to the systematic CA Index Name, the CAS Registry Number and the molecular formula of a ring system.

The Handbook is composed of three parts: the Ring Systems File, the indexes and the supplements.

5.1 Ring Systems File

In the Ring Systems File, containing 60,000 ring systems, the entries are arranged in order of their ring analysis, that means the short description of the cyclic skeletons (cf. 2.1.3, p. 35). Each entry provides the information shown in Fig. 80.

The illustrative structural diagram with the numerical locants on the constituent atoms is particularly helpful when the systematic Index Names of derivatives of the appropriate ring system are sought. With these names a literature search can be rapidly carried out either on-line or in the CAS printed services.

Following the listing of ring systems all the currently known cage structures and metallocenes are given. About 180 substances are arranged alphanumerically according to their molecular formulae.

RING SYSTEMS FILE – 1984 EDITION

① ——————— **6 RINGS: 5,5,6,6,6,6**
$C_3NS–C_5–C_4O_2–C_6–C_6–C_6$

②

③ **RF 52002** 74685–96–4

④ Dispiro[1,3–dioxane–4,17'–[17*H*]cyclopenta[*a*]phe⸗
nanthrene–3'(2'*H*),2"–thiazolidine]

⑤ $C_{22}H_{21}NO_2S$

⑥ L E5 B666 FX OX PHJ F–& AT6XO DOT⸗
J& O–& BT5MXSTJ

⑦ CA 93:47011q

⑧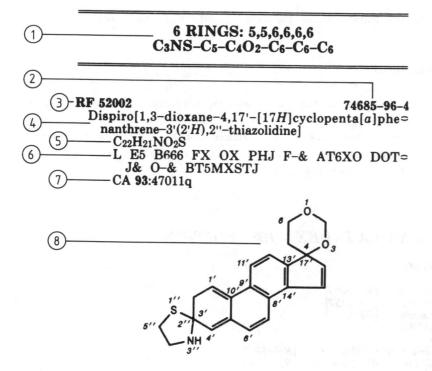

Fig. 80: Excerpt from the Ring Systems File

1. Ring analysis: number of component rings, ring sizes and elemental analysis of the component rings
2. CAS Registry Number
3. Sequential Ring File Number
4. Latest CA Index Name
5. Molecular formula
6. Wiswesser Line notation: a computer-readable description of the structure of a substance – in contrast to the CAS Registry Number which contains no structural information
7. Volume and abstract number of the CA abstract in which the substance was first described
8. The structural diagram with numerical locants

5.2 Index to the Ring Systems Handbook

The index to the Ring Systems Handbook consists of two parts:

Ring Formula Index

The Ring Formula Index to the Ring Systems Handbook is arranged alpha-numerically according to the molecular formulae of the ring systems. Individual ring systems are grouped under a molecular formula according to their ring analysis (Fig. 81). The systematic CA Index Names and the Ring File Number are given.

RING FORMULA INDEX – 1984 EDITION

C₇NS : 1 RING
  C₇NS
    1,3–Thiazonine   *[RF 2456]*
    1,4–Thiazonine   *[RF 2457]*
    1,5–Thiazonine   *[RF 2458]*
C₇NS : 2 RINGS
  C₂NS–C₆
    1–Thia–2–azaspiro[3.5]nonane   *[RF 4887]*
    1–Thia–3–azaspiro[3.5]nonane   *[RF 4888]*
  C₂NS–C₆N
    9–Thia–1–azabicyclo[5.2.0]nonane   *[RF 5078]*
  C₃N–C₅NS
    4–Thia–1–azabicyclo[5.2.0]nonane   *[RF 5093]*
    6–Thia–1–azabicyclo[5.2.0]nonane   *[RF 5094]*
  C₃N–C₅S
    7–Thia–1–azaspiro[3.5]nonane   *[RF 4963]*

Fig. 81: Excerpt from the Ring Formula Index to the Ring Systems Handbook

Ring Name Index

All the systematic CA Index Names – with references to the corresponding Ring File Numbers – are listed alphabetically in the Ring Name Index (Fig. 82). In this case, as they are only the names of parent compounds, inversion of the CA Index Names is impossible.

RING NAME INDEX – 1984 EDITION

1–Boratricyclo[3.1.0.0^{2,6}]hexane   [*RF 12201*]
3–Boratricyclo[4.3.1.1^{3,8}]undecane   [*RF 25177*]
Borazine   [*RF 955*]
Borecin   [*RF 2651*]
Borepane   [*RF 1944*]
1*H*–Borepin   [*RF 1945*]
2*H*–Borepino[2,3–*b*:7,6–*b*']dithiophene   [*RF 17918*]
2*H*–Borepino[3,2–*b*:6,7–*b*']dithiophene   [*RF 17919*]
3*H*–Borepino[2,3–*c*:6,7–*c*']dithiophene   [*RF 17920*]
Boretane   [*RF 238*]
Borete   [*RF 239*]

Fig. 82: Excerpt from the Ring Name Index to the Ring Systems Handbook

Cumulative supplements with an arrangement analagous to that of the
main Handbook are issued twice a year. In addition, they include a cumulative list of all structures for which the data have changed since
the main Handbook was issued.

RING SYSTEMS FILE – 1984 EDITION

---

4 RINGS: 6,6,6,7
C₅N–C₆–C₆–C₅N₂

$$C_5N{-}C_6{-}C_6{-}C_5N_2$$

RF 39344   **54499–23–9**
1*H*–Benzo[*f*][1,2]diazepino[3,4–*b*]quinoline
  C₁₆H₁₁N₃
  T D7 B666 HNN KN SHJ
  CA 81:169520c

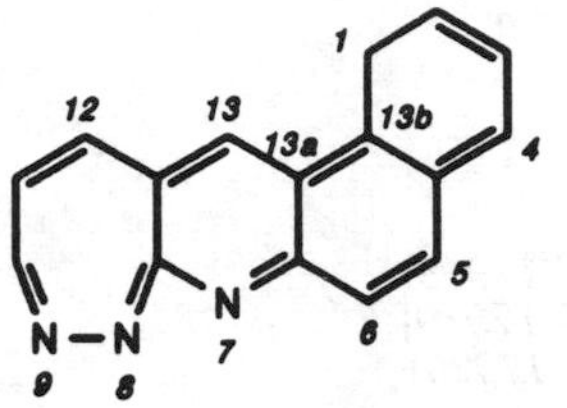

Fig. 83: Excerpt from the Ring System File

5.3 Sample search: What was published about the following ring system
up to and including 1983?

To illustrate: Ring Systems Handbook
Chemical Substance Index

As the systematic CA Index Name of this substance is unknown, and de-
riving it is too exacting, it can be determined with the help of the
Ring Systems Handbook. The ring analysis is:

4-Ring System

6,6,6,7

$C_5N-C_6-C_6-C_5N_2$

The Ring Systems File (Fig. 83) not only provides the systematic CA
Index Name, with which the literature search can be continued in the
Chemical Abstracts volume indexes, but also shows the abstract number
in which the substance was first reported (Chemical Abstracts Volume
81 published in 1974).

1972–1976 CHEM. SUBSTANCE INDEX

1*H*–Benzo[*f*][1,2]diazepino[3,4–*b*]quinoline
   [*54499–23–9*]

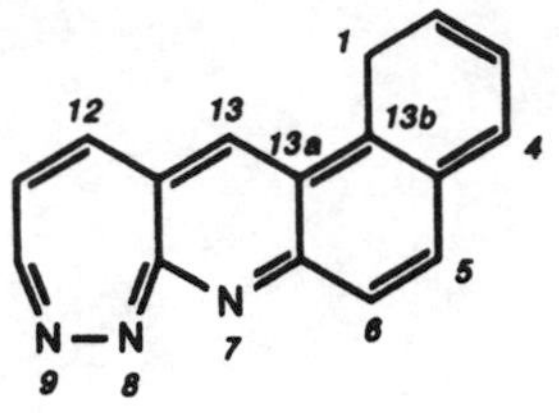

12 13 13a 13b 1
N—N 9 8 7 6 5 4

1*H*–Benzo[*f*][1,2]diazepino[4,3–*c*]quinoline
   [*54499–22–8*]

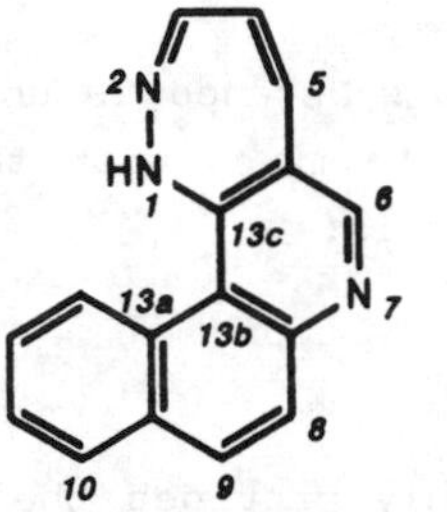

2 N 5
HN 1 13c 6
13a 13b N 7
10 9 8

——, **3,5,6–trimethyl–** [*54226–54–9*]
   prepn. and cyclization of, 81: 169520c

Fig. 84: Excerpt from the Chemical Substance Index to the 9th collec-
          tive period

In the Ninth Collective Chemical Substance Index, which covers the period from 1972 to 1976, the structure of the substance in the problem can be easily identified using the substance name and the CAS Registry Number. The structure diagram and numerical locants of every substance included in the Ring Systems Handbook is illustrated in the Chemical Substance Index to Chemical Abstracts.

No abstract number is cited for the actual ring system itself in the Chemical Substance Index. This indicates that the non-substituted substance was not the subject of a paper. Only one derivative of this ring system is mentioned.

Before the search is continued in the Tenth Collective Index for the period from 1977 to 1981, the Index Guide should be consulted to ascertain whether the systematic CA Index Name is also valid for this collective period. As the substance name is not mentioned in the Index Guide, the Chemical Substance Index to the tenth collective period can be immediately consulted. But no entry is to found there. The search in the CA volume indexes up to 1983 also proved to be fruitless.

This means that the ring system in the problem has only been mentioned once, i.e. in 1974, in the literature up to and including 1983.

6 Computer-Readable Services of the Chemical Abstracts Service

As a supplement to their printed information, the Chemical Abstracts Service provides some of its services in the form of computer-readable files, others are available only as computer files. These services are supplied on magnetic tape. The information is stored on the magnetic tape in the Standard Distribution Format (SDF) which was jointly developed by the Chemical Abstracts Service and its users. Each single piece of information, e.g. the title of a publication, the Index Name, the molecular formula or a subject term, is stored as a defined unit whose structure is constant. As a result, a suitable computer program can be used to select information from a large number of precisely defined data elements on the magnetic tape as an aid for subsequent searches, i.e. to define what should, and what should not, be researched.

There are three possible ways of making use of the computer-readable files of the Chemical Abstracts Service:

1. The computer-readable services can be directly leased from the Chemical Abstracts Service and processed with the user's own computer. However, the necessary software for searches must be developed by the user himself. Compared with other methods of use, this is often the most expensive solution nowadays.

2. It is possible to address a problem to an information broker or an information centre (e.g. Fachinformationszentrum Chemie, Berlin; Royal Society of Chemistry, Nottingham; Centre National de l'Information Chimique, Paris; Japan Association for International Chemical Information, Tokyo). This method is especially advantageous when only occasional searches in the information material of the Chemical Abstracts Service are to be carried out.

3. A searcher can take advantage of access to databases offered by hosts (database vendors) who have, for their part, stored all or part of the CAS computer-readable material in their computer using their own computer programs and who make this material available for online searches. In this case the customer is directly linked to the computer of the database supplier via a data transmission network, or the postal telecommunication system, by means of his own data terminal e.g. a telex machine, a terminal or a microcomputer. As the importance of these online searches is growing every day, they will be dealt with in detail in chapters 7, 8 and 9 (p.135, 146 and 207).

6.1 CA SEARCH

CA SEARCH is the most important magnetic tape service offered by the Chemical Abstracts Service, as it is almost equivalent to the printed version of Chemical Abstracts. CA SEARCH is issued every week like the Chemical Abstracts journal and the following information is stored on magnetic tape:
- all the bibliographic data contained in Chemical Abstracts including the complete title of the original publication
- all the keywords extracted from CA abstracts, and their titles, which were included in the CA issue indexes
- all entries in the CA volume indexes, extracted from the original document including the text modifications, i.e. the complete contents of the General Subject Index, the Chemical Subject Index and the Formula Index.

N.B. CA SEARCH does not include CA abstract texts.

In CA SEARCH the following terms can be retrieved:
- trivial names, trade names and semi-systematic substance names
- systematic CA Index Names
- molecular formulae
- CAS Registry Numbers
- classes of compounds
- general subject terms and
- chemical procedures and processes.

One particular advantage of CA SEARCH compared with searches in the printed version of CA is that a search can be carried out using search terms which are either:
- part of a controlled vocabulary which must be used for searching in the printed version of Chemical Abstracts
  or
- from the common vocabulary, i.e. natural language phrases. This is not possible in the printed version.
CA SEARCH has been available since 1980; similar services, differently named, have been offered since 1967.

6.2 Registry Nomenclature Service (RNS)

There is no CAS printed equivalent to the Registry Nomenclature Service. This computer file consists of part of the information stored according to the CAS Registry System (cf. 1.3,   p. 4 and chap. 4, p. 108), i.e. all of the almost 8.4 million substances, including more than 12 million substance names, which have been cited in Chemical Abstracts up to now. The following data are made available for each substance and all are retrievable:
- CAS Registry Number
- molecular formula
- systematic CA Index Name
- stereochemical descriptors
- all known trivial, trade and semi-systematic names.

No information about the structure of the substances is contained in the Registry Nomenclature Service. This service is issued every month and includes data describing approximately 50,000 new substances which have been registered in the CA Registry System in the previous four weeks.

All substances mentioned in the literature from 1965 onwards, as well as most of those mentioned in the period between 1957 and 1964, have been stored and are retrievable.

6.3 Registry Structure Service (RSS)

The computer-readable Registry Structure Service supplements the Registry Nomenclature Service and contains information about the structural diagrams of 8.4 million substances. Like the RNS, this computer-readable service has no printed equivalent. The following data are stored for each substance:
- CAS Registry Number
- the topological connection tables of the individual atoms for the two-dimensional structure
- the stereochemical descriptors, labelled atoms and uncommon valences.

The Registry Structure Service also appears monthly with the connection tables of the most recently reported substances (approx. 50,000).

6.4 Other CAS Computer-Readable Services

The following services are exactly equivalent to the printed versions
and a detailed description of what they offer can be read in the appropriate chapters of this book.

CA Index Guide: this machine-readable service contains all the information from the alphabetical part of the Index Guide (cf. 2.1.2, p.21).

CAS Source Index: identical to the printed edition of CASSI including
the supplements (cf. 3.1, p. 100).

Chemical–Biological Activities (CBAC): contains all the information in
Chemical Abstracts from Sections 1 to 5 and 62 to 64 (cf. 2.1.1, p.
14, 15).

Polymer Science and Technology (POST): contains all the information in
Chemical Abstracts from Sections 35 to 46 (cf. 2.1.1, p. 15).

Chemical Industry Notes (CIN): is equivalent to the printed edition of
the journal "Chemical Industry Notes". CIN contains brief, informative
extracts from 80 leading industry and trade journals. Its primary aims
are to present economic developments in the chemical industry and
facilitate decisions on management, investments, and sales and produc-
tion planning.
The CIN abstracts are grouped into eight subject sections:
- Production
- Pricing
- Sales
- Facilities
- Products and Activities
- Corporate Activities
- Government Activities
- People in the Chemical Industry.

It is possible to search for all the keywords from the headings of the
CIN abstracts, all the names of persons and of companies and corporations.

Like the printed edition, the computer-readable form of CIN is issued
weekly.

Chemical Titles (CT): is equivalent to the journal "Chemical Titles". The computer-readable service contains the titles of all the papers included in about 800 of the most important chemical journals and informs chemists and chemical engineers about the latest advances in theory and practice approximately a month before the abstracts appear in Chemical Abstracts.

All the keywords from the titles of the publications are searchable. On average each heading contains seven keywords (in the printed edition the permutated headings are listed in the alphabetical order of the keywords). In addition, the complete bibliographic data, including the CODEN, and the authors' names are retrievable.

The computer-readable form of Chemical Titles - like the journal - is issued every two weeks.

7 Online Access to the Databases of the Chemical Abstracts Service

7.1 Technical Requirements

Fig. 85 shows a schematic illustration of the three components necessary for an online search: data terminal, communication device and the
host computer with its databases.

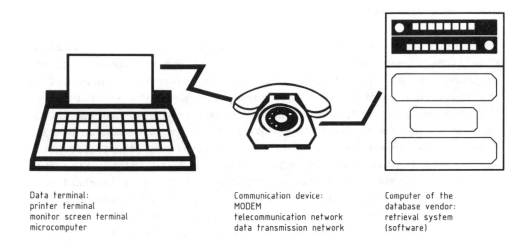

Data terminal:
printer terminal
monitor screen terminal
microcomputer

Communication device:
MODEM
telecommunication network
data transmission network

Computer of the
database vendor:
retrieval system
(software)

Fig. 85: Technical set-up for an online search

The simplest **data terminal** is a printer terminal. Even using such
simple equipment, structure diagrams can be retrieved by entering the
structure or structural fragment on the keyboard in the form of letter
codes (text structure input). These commands are converted by the host
computer software into a searchable form. The answer in the form of a
structure diagram is given out by the printer. As printers work relatively slowly, searches using such terminals are rather time-consuming. Before the input question can be revised or supplemented, the
searcher must wait until the result, whether in the form of bibliographic data or structure diagram, has been printed.

The second group of data terminals which can be used are monitor
screen terminals. However, an additional printer is certainly advisable. In this case the search results can be directly scanned on the
screen and, if necessary, the search question modified at once. As it

is not necessary to wait for a printed result, the dialogue can be speeded up.

Today microcomputers are increasingly used as data terminals. However, in this case it is essential that the microcomputer is equipped to carry on a dialogue with the help of special computer programs, which are also commercially available. Some microcomputers, which can process special graphic software (for CAS ONLINE: Tektronix Plot 10), are capable of showing the specified structure diagram, entered by means of text structure input, on the monitor or even to process a structure drawn on a data tablet.

The second important component for an online search is the **communication link** between the searcher's own terminal and the computer of the database vendor. Special data transmission networks are provided by the individual countries for this purpose, e.g. in the Federal Republic of Germany DATEX-P, the European Economic Community provides EURONET and in the U.S.A. TELENET or TYMNET. These networks can be dialled from a normal telephone. However, a user's permit is required from the appropriate organization. As only analogue signals (alternating current) can be transmitted by these networks, but the data terminal only emits digital signals (direct current) a MODEM (MOdulator/DEModulator) or an acoustic coupler must be inserted between the data terminal and the transmission network for the necessary signal conversion.

Thus, the transmission network gives access to the **database vendor** (host), from whom permission to use the service must also be obtained in advance. The database vendor is usually a commercial organization which provides access to numerous databases – in one case 160 different ones (DIALOG). These databases are only rarely compiled by the host itself, in most cases they are bought or leased by the vendor. The information is obtained on magnetic tape, processed and fed into the host's own computer so that a database becomes searchable. In order to use this database it is essential to have a precise knowledge of the organization program and search program, the retrieval system and the command language of the host, as almost every database vendor has devised his own system. The disadvantage of having to learn different command languages is compensated for by the fact that the various commands also comprise a variety of different questions. The answers can supplement each other and thus enable a more complete literature search.

7.2 Hosts who offer access to the databases of the Chemical Abstracts
    Service

There are a total of eight organizations around the world which offer
access to the data material of the Chemical Abstracts Service:

1. STN International

CAS databases are called CAS ONLINE with three Files: CA File (similar
to CA SEARCH, but it contains the CA abstract texts), Registry File
(RNS and RSS) and CAOLD File (cf. 7.3, p. 141); from 1988 two additional files will be available: CASREACT and CApreviews (cf. 7.3, p.
142)

    a in North America:
      STN International
      2540 Olentangy River Road
      P.O. Box 02228
      Columbus, Ohio 43202, U.S.A.
      Phone: (614) 421-3600   Telex: 6842 086 chmab

    b in Europe
      STN International Karlsruhe
      Postfach 24 65
      D-7500 Karlsruhe 1
      Phone: (0049) 7247/824568   Telex: 17724710+

    c in Japan
      STN International
      c/o Japan Association for International Chemical Information
      Gakkai Center Building
      2-4-16 Yayoi, Bungyo-ku
      Tokyo 113, Japan
      Phone: 03-816-3462   Telex: 2 723 805 JAICI.J

2.   Télésystème Questel
      83-85, Boulvard Vincent Auriol
      F-75013 Paris, France
      Phone: (00331) 45826464
      CAS databases: CA SEARCH, RSS

3.   DATA-STAR
      Radio Schweiz A.G.
      Laupenstr. 18
      CH-3008 Bern, Switzerland
      Phone: (0041) 31 659500
      CAS databases: CA SEARCH, RNS, CIN

4.   ESA-IRS
      European Space Agency - Information Retrieval Service
      Via Galileo Galilei
      I-00044 Frascati, Italy
      Phone: (0039) 69 4011
      CAS databases: CA SEARCH

5.   National Library of Medicine
      BL 38 R-C6B Rockville Pike
      Bethesda Md. 20014, U.S.A.
      CAS databases: CA SEARCH,
      CBAC, Index Guide

6.   SDC Search Service
      System Development Corporation
      2500 Colorado Avenue
      Santa Monica, California 90406, U.S.A.
      Phone: 213/453-6194
      CAS databases: CA SEARCH, RNS, CIN

7.   DIALOG Information Retrieval Service
      3460 Hillview Avenue
      Palo Alto, California 94304, U.S.A.
      Phone: (800) 227-1960
      CAS databases: CA SEARCH, RNS, Index Guide, CIN
                     (In addition, CA SEARCH contains ring
                     information which is searchable)

8.   BRS Information Service
      1350 Ave. of Americas
      Suite 1802
      New York 10019, U.S.A.
      Phone: 800/2454
      CAS databases: CA SEARCH

All hosts offer access to CA SEARCH, but not necessarily under that name. Depending on the structure of the host's computer, the information can be contained in a single file or, for instance, divided into five files corresponding to the collective periods - as in the case of SDC. As each of these hosts has devised their own command language (except where different hosts cooperate), the data material has been processed in different ways and it is possible that a searcher will obtain different answers to the same basic question. In order to ensure that a literature search is really thorough, it is sometimes advisable to consult the data from different hosts. The searcher must, however, be familiar with the details of the dialogue language and also know how the data of the Chemical Abstracts Service was processed. But, as the competition between the hosts is quite fierce, future development of software will not stop. Thus, the different retrieval command languages are becoming increasingly similar.

All eight hosts offer access to nomenclature files which were developed from the Registry Nomenclature Service. Some of the nomenclature files contain all the 8.4 million substances and the 12 million substance names. Some offer extracts from the data e.g. a file with all substance names which were mentioned only once and a file with the names of substances which were mentioned at least twice in the literature (DIALOG).

Only two hosts offer the online user the possibility of searching for structure diagrams: Télésystème Questel and STN International. By entering a substance name, no matter how complex, the chemist can have a structure diagram displayed within seconds. Or he can start with a structure diagram and just as rapidly receive the systematic CA Index Name (without having to worry about nomenclature problems) and, in addition, the CAS Registry Number and all available trivial and trade names. However, the great advantage of these structure databases - and no printed service can offer anything comparable - is the possibility of searches using structure fragments. Thus, a substructure, with clearly marked positions where substitution can take place and where substituents are impossible, can be entered. The structure diagrams with the appropriate CAS Registry Numbers and CA Index Names of the substances which contain these substructures are then retrieved from the database.

Fig. 86 is a schematic illustration of the relationship between the original publication, the printed and computer-readable services of CAS and the database vendors.

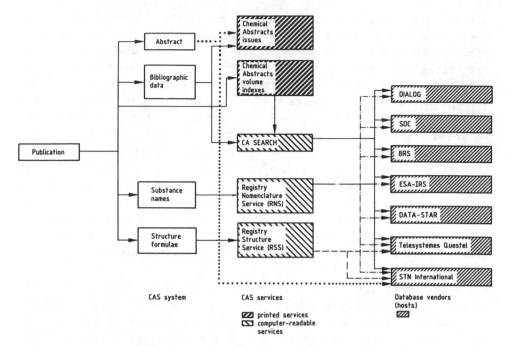

Fig. 86: Relationship between the printed and the computer-readable
         CAS services

Which of the available databases a searcher should use depends on the
technical set-up at his disposal and on the questions he wishes to
pose. When choosing, it is always important to consider which other
databases the host has to offer, as databases containing certain
facts, e.g. spectra, can be a helpful supplement to literature searches in the field of chemistry. On the other hand, it is often advisable when searching in related fields, e.g. of physical chemistry, to
search in the databases of physics as well. If a searcher is very familiar with the command language of a host as a result of frequent
searches, e.g. in economic databases, he will prefer this host. Before
embarking on an online search the user should have precise information
on which databases the host offers.

7.3 CAS ONLINE or the Chemical Abstracts Service as a Host

The Chemical Abstracts Service is one of the few organizations which allows general access to its own self-compiled information material for online searches. It is therefore both a database producer and vendor. Thus, the Chemical Abstracts Service offers several advantages over other hosts.

Its own data files are called CAS ONLINE. The Chemical Abstracts Service offers access to three different files at the moment:
- CA File
- Registry File
- CAOLD File
From 1988 onwards two additional files will be accessible:
- CASREACT
- CApreviews

The **CA File** not only includes all the information on the magnetic tape service CA SEARCH, i.e. the complete bibliographic data since 1967, but also - and this is the point which makes CAS vastly superior to all other hosts who offer CA SEARCH - all abstract texts published in Chemical Abstracts since 1970 (CA Volume 72, January 1970). Thus, the CA File is identical with Chemical Abstracts. The CA File now contains 6.3 million abstract texts for online searching and the bibliographic and index data of 7.6 million records.

The **Registry File** contains 8.4 million structure diagrams together with the corresponding CAS Registry Numbers, the molecular formulae and 12 million substance names. The Registry File is linked to the CA File through the Registry Number, i.e. it is possible to continue a search in the CA File and locate bibliographic information and abstract texts using the CAS Registry Number obtained from the Registry File. The Registry Numbers can also be combined with other concepts like subject terms, authors' names, CA Section Numbers as well as other CAS Registry Numbers in the CA File.

The **CAOLD File** is in the process of being compiled and covers almost all abstracts between 1957 and 1966 (i.e. the sixth and seventh collective periods) not included in the CA File. The Chemical Abstracts Service is continuously adding chemical substances indexed prior to 1965 to the CAOLD File. Thus, when literature about a substance published prior to 1967 is sought, the CAS Registry Number found in the Registry File is transferred to CAOLD where the CA abstract numbers or the CA accession numbers can be found. As abstracts were formerly not awarded individual numbers in Chemical Abstracts (cf. 2.8, p. 97), the column numbers (CA accession numbers) are given. If desired, the CAS Registry Numbers of further substances which are also mentioned in that particular CA abstract can be listed.

The Chemical Abstracts Service has announced that two additional CAS ONLINE files will be offered from 1988 onwards: CASREACT and CApreviews.

CASREACT is an information service containing data about chemical reactions. Searches can be carried out with structures, substructures or CAS Registry Numbers. It is possible to specify the role of a substance in a reaction, e.g. whether it is a reactant, a product, a solvent or a catalyst. The search result shows the reaction diagram with the CA abstract number or abstract text. The contents of the file is drawn from articles published in over 100 key journals since January 1985. Initially, the file will contain about 500,000 reactions, and about 170,000 reactions will be added each year.

The **CApreviews** file provides bibliographic data of documents which have not yet been added to the CA File. This information can be obtained by the user six to eight weeks earlier than was previously possible in CAS ONLINE searches. The file is searchable using terms such as title, corporate source, and authors' names; the search result includes the title and bibliographic information of the journal article, patent, or report of interest.

Another point which distinguishes the Chemical Abstracts Service from other hosts is that CAS is part of a data communication network system: STN International (Scientific and Technical Information Network) which is jointly offered by CAS in Columbus/Ohio, U.S.A., FIZ Karlsruhe (Fachinformationszentrum Energie, Physik, Mathematik) in Karlsruhe, Federal Republic of Germany and Japan Information Center of Science and Technology (JICST) in Tokyo, Japan. The computers of these three service centres are linked through STN so that a file is mounted only on one computer in this network. However, it is possible to access each individual file from every service centre in the association. Thus, users from Europe can dial STN Karlsruhe and are automatically connected to the computer in Columbus if they wish to carry out a search in the CAS ONLINE Files. Only the telephone costs for the connection with Karlsruhe are charged, there is no additional charge for the link with Columbus. Online users in the U.S.A. access STN via the service centre in Columbus, and when they wish to search the file Physics Briefs, which is loaded on the computer in Karlsruhe, they are automatically connected to this service centre by keying the command PHYS.

Fig. 87 shows the search terms which can be used to obtain information from the various CAS ONLINE Files and the appropriate answers.

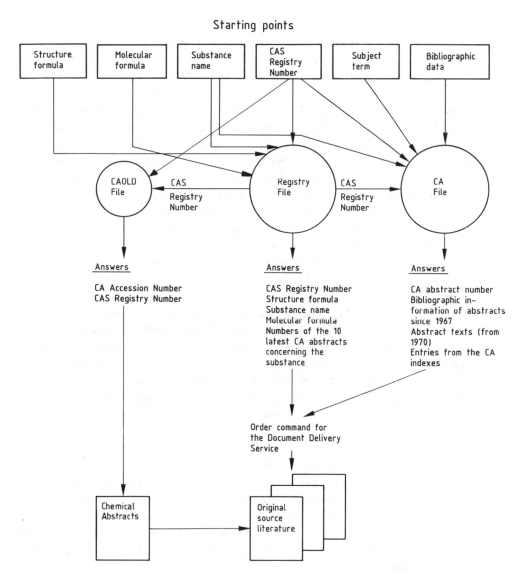

Fig. 87: Searching in CAS ONLINE Files

7.4 Search Aids for Online Users

Several aids, which are important for literature searches in the printed services, have a similar significance for online searches. They
are especially useful for ascertaining search terms and for devising
search profiles, e.g.:
- the Index Guide (cf. 2.1.2, p. 21)
- the Subject Coverage Manual, the 1975, 1982 and 1987 editions (cf.
  2.1.1, p. 17).

CAS offers the following aids especially for searches in CA SEARCH -
regardless of which host provides the service:
- Natural Language Term List: an alphabetical list of all single words
  which have appeared five or more times in the abstract titles and
  keyword indexes of Vols. 78 to 81 and 86 to 89. The list helps the
  user to select terms and to determine when and where to truncate
  them. It also provides access to embedded word stems and gives frequencies for each term. So the user may find additional search
  terms and may estimate how many answers a search term will offer.
- Rotated Title Phrase List: here all multiword phrases from document
  titles are compiled and the list also gives frequencies for each
  phrase in document titles from CA SEARCH Vols. 78 to 81. As the
  phrases are listed alphabetically for each single keyword, it is
  easy to recognize the combination in which search terms can occur.
- CA Headings List: this aid is divided into two parts: general subject headings and plant and animal headings. The most important
  terms from the controlled vocabulary of the General Subject Index
  (valid for the ninth, tenth and eleventh collective periods, i.e.
  1972 up to 1987) are included in this directory. Furthermore, the
  list gives cross-references which link the subject terms used in
  one collective period with the valid terms in other collective periods. Similarly, natural language descriptions are referred to valid terms in the controlled vocabulary.

In addition, the hosts themselves often issue comprehensive written
information, containing details of the special command language on the
one hand, and describing the contents and organization of the individual databases on the other. These manuals are sometimes very specialized and can often be completely understood and used only by searchers
with some experience in online searches. However, almost every host
offers one or two-day introductory workshops which are especially
useful for beginners.

Especially for CAS ONLINE files the Chemical Abstracts Service offers
a variety of user aids for novices and experienced searchers:
- STN International: A Guide to Commands and Databases
- Using the Learning Files
- Using CAS ONLINE: The CA File
- Using CAS ONLINE: The Registry File
- CAS ONLINE Screen Dictionary
- Adding Screens in Structure Searching
- Structuring Functional Groups
- Specifying Bonds in Structures
- Searching Coordinate Compounds.

A detailed description of the currently available aids for CA SEARCH
and CAS ONLINE is contained in the annual CAS International Catalog
available in English, German, French and Japanese.

8 Using CAS ONLINE
Author: H.R.Pichler

8.1 Indroductory Remarks

8.1.1 Special Features of CAS ONLINE

In the following chapter the important steps and commands for searching CAS ONLINE will be explained and demonstrated using examples.
Besides the Files described in 7.3 (p. 141) CAS ONLINE offers two very
inexpensive training files:

- LCA File

  The LCA File is an excerpt from the CA File and contains approximately 65,000 CA abstracts. It is searchable exactly like
  the CA File, but no offline printouts are possible.

- LREG File

  The LREG File is an excerpt from the Registry File and contains
  approximately 100,000 chemical substances. It is searchable in the
  same way as the Registry File. However, offline printouts are not
  possible.

Only an hourly rate for the computer link is charged for each of these
training files i.e. $ 30,- per hour. The telecommunications charges
are, of course, extra.

A further special feature of searching in CAS ONLINE should be explained in advance. During the login procedure the user is asked to
identify the type of terminal he is using. There are three alternatives:

1. HP 2647 terminal specially equipped with the CAS ONLINE Graphic
   Structure Input programme (GSI). The HP 2647 was the only terminal
   with this convenient menu selection technique which could be used
   to create the structure of the substance being sought. However,
   since Hewlett Packard does not manufacture this terminal any more,
   it is no longer emphasized by CAS.

2. A Tektronix-compatible graphics terminal for text structure input
   and graphic input and retrieval of structure diagrams. Users who
   prefer a graphic input of the desired structure rather than the
   text structure input have two alternatives:

   a) The DRAW command

      The structure is drawn on the screen by moving the cursor. All
      other details (atoms, bond value and type) must be entered as
      text.

b) Menu selection

This method allows structures to be generated on the screen by combining individual structural components – e.g. rings and C-chains. The individual components of the structure are selected from a table (Fig. 88) using the cursor. The DRAW command is integrated into the menu technique. A combination of this method and text structure input is also possible. The menu selection on the second type of terminal is not identical to that on the HP 2647 terminal, but they are similar in practice.

3. Non-graphic, asynchronous terminals for text structure input. Even on this type of terminal CAS ONLINE software enables the output of structure diagrams when searches are carried out in the Registry File. However, their quality is inferior to those generated on type 1 and 2.

```
                                        HELP    KEY
                                        SHIFT   END
                                        RECALL
                                        REFRESH
                                        SHORTCUTS
                                        C1   C2   C3
                                        C4   C5   C6
                                        R4   R5   R6
                                        R7   R8   GRAPH
                                        C    N    O
                                        Si   P    S
                                        F    Cl   Br
                                        X    M    Gk.
                                        A    Q    NODE
                                        S    SE   N
                                        D    DE   T
                                        UNSPEC BOND
                                        R    C    RC
                                        CHARGE  MASS
                                        HCOUNT  NSPEC
                                        VALENCE RSPEC
R=Refresh, S=Select, K=Key, F=From, T=To, M=Move, D=Delete
```

Fig. 88: CAS menu selection for creating a structure using graphic input

Types 1 and 2 are intended for searches in the Registry File, while all asynchronous terminals, whether they are monitor screens or simple printer terminals, are suitable for searches in the text files. Type 3 can be indicated in every case regardless of which terminal is actually used. Two differences become apparent to the user when searching in the CA and CAOLD Files:

Type 2: The system has a Tektronix output mode, i.e. a screenful at a time. A prompt saying "COPY AND CLEAR PAGE, PLEASE" appears at the end of each full screen. If desired, the contents of the screen should be copied and then the screen cleared using the appropriate key. Otherwise the subsequent text will be written over the existing one, thus rendering it unreadable. The "COPY AND CLEAR PAGE" prompt is a nuisance when a structure search in the Registry File is continued in the CA File, as it repeatedly interupts the text. This prompt can be suppressed by the "SET PAGE LENGTH SCROLL" command. If the search should return to the graphic mode the command "SET PAGE LENGTH 33" must be entered. The original situation (with graphics) is automatically restored when logging off. However, "SET PAGE LENGTH SCROLL" is only to be recommended when the terminal can be switched from the graphic to the alpha mode. Some types, for example the older Tektronix 4014 models, are incapable of scrolling, i.e. continuous displaying of the text. As soon as the screen is full the subsequent text is superimposed on the existing text, as there is no "COPY AND CLEAR PAGE" command to halt the text.

Type 3: the text is continuously dispatched, the prompt "COPY AND CLEAR PAGE, PLEASE" is omitted. Structure diagrams can be displayed, but their quality is poorer. The output of structure diagrams can be suppressed by the command "SET GRAPHICS OFF". All other information is given. This is also valid for terminal types 1 and 2.

As mentioned above, the CAOLD File contains references to publications which appeared in Chemical Abstracts before 1967. The contents of the CAOLD File differ considerably from those of the CA File, as it consists of only two or three fields per unit (cf. 8.10, p. 205) i.e the accession number (AN), index terms (IT; in this case only the CAS Registry Number) and the document type (DT) if it is a patent. However, this information is sufficient to locate the abstract texts and bibliographic details by way of the printed edition of Chemical Abstracts. Searches are possible using only the CAS Registry Number and - if available - the document type P (patent).

The structure-orientated Registry File is linked to the CA and CAOLD Files making a separate nomenclature file unnecessary. Results of a structure search (in the form of CAS Registry Numbers) can be transferred to the text files and linked to non-structural search terms.

Each time the search is tranferred to another file CAS ONLINE automatically informs the user of the costs incurred:

Cost in U.S. Dollars	Since File Entry	Total Session
Full estimated cost	48.00	48.00
Discounts (for qualifying accounts)		
CA subscriber	-10.36	-10.36

The automatic display can be supressed with the command SET COST OFF.
Thereafter the costs can be recalled at any time using the command
DISPLAY COST or the automatic display switched on again with SET COST
ON.

8.1.2 Login Procedure

The details of the login procedure vary depending on the locality from
which the user is attempting to access STN. Login cards giving complete details are available from STN Columbus.

After logging in the user is prompted by the system:

>   Welcome to STN International! Please Enter x:

Enter "X"

>   X twice in succession and press the RETURN key

Now the user is requested to enter:

>   LOGINID:XXXXXXXX   The user's account number and pass-
>   word, identifications awarded to the
>   PASSWORD:YYYYYYYY   user when he opens an account with
>   STN, are entered.

>   TERMINAL (ENTER 1,2,3 or ?): Enter 3 (cf. 8.1.1 for
>   explanation)

This login procedure can be entered consecutively in one line directly after the "LOGINID" prompt as follows:

        XXXXXXXX YYYYYYYY 3

The welcome message from CAS ONLINE appears

        ****** Welcome to STN International ******

followed by some introductory information and subsequently the message

        FILE "H O M E" ENTERED AT 03:21:14 ON 30 JAN 87

The system automatically connects the user with the Login File "HOME". This is a kind of "antechamber" to the data files and offers news about the databases (NEWS) or information about the command language (HELP).

8.2 Searching the Registry File

This file is based on topological connection tables which CAS has set up for each registered substance. Each atom of a chemical substance is written into a kind of table and its neighbouring atoms, as well as the types of bonds connecting them, are precisely specified. The computer program converts the query structure into such a table and compares it with those already filed.

8.2.1 Generating the Query Structure

The structure in question is generated with the aid of specific commands, the most important of which will be presented in the following. The structure diagrams were produced on a simple type 3 terminal (non-graphic) in this case.

GRA (Graph)

The basic skeleton of the substance is created with this command. It should be noted that the individual atoms are numbered by the system. Although this usually happens in a predictable sequence, it is often advisable, especially for the inexperienced searcher, to build up the skeleton step by step from its component parts. The DIS command allows the searcher to view the structure at any time to ensure that, for instance, substituents on rings or chains have really been placed in the correct position.

GRA C4 generates a chain of 4 carbon atoms, whereby C stands for chain and not carbon. The basic skeleton is, however, also built up of carbon atoms unless otherwise specified. Hydrogen is not included in the basic skeleton.

```
C?????C????C?????C
1     2    3     4
```

GRA C6,3 C2,5 C2 produces a branched carbon chain. C6 specifies a chain of six carbon atoms, the remainder of the entry adds two C2 chains branching from the 3rd and 5th atom. As shown, the system numbers the atoms consecutively in the order of their input:

```
        8              10
        C              C
        ?              ?
        ?              ?
        ?              ?
        C   7          C   9
        ?              ?
        ?              ?
C?????C????C?????C????C?????C
1     2    3     4    5     6
```

GRA R6 produces a ring consisting of 6 carbon atoms. The atoms are numbered clockwise:

```
        2
        C
1    ?     ?    3
  C?         ? C
  ?            ?
  ?            ?
  C            C
6    ?     ?    4
     ? C?
        5
```

GRA R66 generates a fused ring system consisting of two C6 rings:

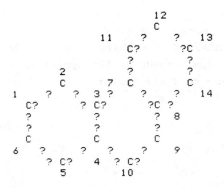

```
         2             7
         C             C
1    ?      ?    3 ?       ?    8
   C?         ? C?          ?C
   ?             ?          ?
   ?             ?          ?
   C             C          C
6    ?       ?       ?        ?    9
     ? C?     4   ? C?
       5            10
```

GRA R66U6 produces the following structure (U stands for up):

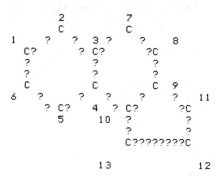

```
                       12
                       C
              11   ?      ?   13
                   C?        ?C
                   ?          ?
          2        ?          ?
          C    7   C          C
1    ?       ? 3 ?    ?      ?    14
   C?         ? C?         ?C ?
   ?             ?          ?  ? 8
   ?             ?          ?
   C             C          C
6    ?       ?       ?       ?    9
     ? C?     4   ? C?
       5            10
```

GRA R66D5 produces the following basic skeleton (D stands for down):

```
         2             7
         C             C
1    ?      ?    3 ?       ?    8
   C?         ? C?          ?C
   ?             ?          ?
   ?             ?          ?
   C             C          C  9
6    ?      ?       ?       ?    ?    11
     ? C?     4   ? C?          ?C
       5         10  ?          ?
                     ?          ?
                     C????????C

              13              12
```

GRA R6,2 C4 generates a C6 ring with a C4 substituent chain on atom number 2:

```
   7
     C????C?????C?????C
     ?     8    9    10
     ?
   2 C
1    ?     ?       3
  C?        ? C
  ?          ?
  ?          ?
  C          C
6   ?      ?    4
    ? C?
    5
```

NOD (Node)

The NOD command defines atoms other than carbon in the structure. Any chemical element or element symbol can be used with the exception of hydrogen, the only single atom which cannot be explicitly specified. In addition there are four symbols of general validity:

X for a halogen
A for any element except hydrogen
Q for any element except hydrogen and carbon
M for any metal.

Thus, for example, by entering

        NOD 4 6 N

the C6 ring shown above becomes a diazine skeleton with C atoms 4 and 6 replaced by nitrogen:

```
    7
       C????C?????C?????C
       ?     8     9    10
       ?
    2  C
1     ?    ?     3
  C?       ? C
  ?          ?
  ?          ?
  N          N
6     ?    ?     4
    ? C?
      5
```

A maximum of 20 nodes can be alternatively occupied by 2 to 20 different atoms in the structural skeleton. For this purpose an identifing
symbol Gk (k = consecutive numbers) can be assigned to each node with
the NOD command, e.g. G1 for node 10 in the above diagram

        NOD 10 G1

G1 stands for a set of up to 20 atoms which alternatively occupy this
position. Any element symbol can be used, in this case even hydrogen
which means that the position is not substituted. The above mentioned
general symbols X, A, Q and M are also admissible. The atoms are specified by the command VAR (variable). In this example G1 should represent N, O and S. The input

        VAR G1=N/O/S

alternatively replaces C-atom 10 by nitrogen, oxygen and sulfur:

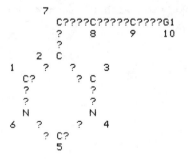

```
    7
       C????C?????C????G1
       ?     8     9    10
       ?
    2  C
1     ?    ?   3
  C?       ? C
  ?          ?
  ?          ?
  N          N
6     ?    ?   4
    ? C?
      5
```

VAR G1=N/O/S

BON (Bonds)

The bonds of a structural skeleton are initially unspecified. The system recognizes the type of bond, i.e. ring or chain bonds, but the
bond value (single, double or triple bonds) must be explicitly stated.
The following symbols are used:

		Display on	Terminal
		Type 2	Type 3
SE	= single exact	C —C	C —C
DE	= double exact	C ═C	C ═C
T	= triple	C ≡C	C ≢C
N	= normalized (aromatic or tautomeric	C ----C	C + C
	according to CAS convention)		
S	= SE or N	C ═══ C	C · C
D	= DE or N	C ═══ C	C : C
U	= unspecified	C ∼∼∼C	C ? C

The bond value "N" requires a detailed explanation as it could very
easily cause difficulty. According to CAS convention it defines an
aromatic or tautomeric bond and this convention differs considerably
from that normally accepted in chemistry. This is more or less a form-
alism which is used when the following conditions are fulfilled:

Tautomerism: A central atom is joined to one of at least two neighbouring atoms by means of a double bond. At least one of
the neighbouring atoms bears a hydrogen atom (or isotope)
or a charge so that a rearrangement of atoms or a charge
transfer can take place.

Scheme:

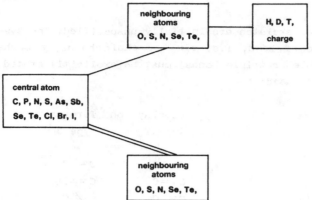

Examples:

non tautomeric	tautomeric

Certain special rules must be noted particularly in the case of charges. These rules can only be understood after careful study of the CAS Structure Conventions (The CAS Chemical Registry System: VII. Tautomerism and Alternating Bonds). In doubtful cases it is advisable to leave the bond value unspecified, or to enter D or S which covers both possibilities.

N.B. The keto-enol tautomeric equilibrium, for instance, does not fit into the above scheme.

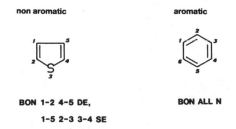

Aromatic Rings: All ring systems with alternating single and double bonds are aromatic. The rings must consist of an even number of atoms.

Example:

At the command level, bonds which are equivalent throughout a ring are indicated by the following entry

        BON R 1 2 N

This means that all bonds in the ring containing atoms 1 and 2 should normalized, i.e. it is aromatic.

BON ALL N,3-4 SE

In this system the bond value N (normalized) applies to the outer ring 1-2-3-6-7-8-4-5-1. It is composed of an even number of atoms, i.e. 8, and the bonds in the outer ring are alternating single and double. Only the bond between atom 3 and 4 is SE (single exact).

NSP (Node Specification)
___

The system recognizes an atom as a ring atom when it is built into a ring and as a chain atom when it is part of a chain. This means that the atom at the terminal position of a chain structure is assumed to be a chain atom when it is further substituted.

Only substances, in which the atom number 10 is part of a chain, would be retrieved as answers when the following structure is entered

for instance

but not

because atom 10 is in a ring in the latter case. If both alternatives are desired then atom 10 must be defined as a ring or a chain atom with the entry "NSP 10 RC" (ring/chain). If only ring structures are required the appropriate entry is NSP 10 R (ring).

This simple node specification is unfortunately impossible for variable groups at present e.g. when atom 10 can be N, O or S alternatively. Each alternative centre must be taken into account when building up the structure. The following example explains how this is done.

```
               ⎛N⟨
C-C-C - ⎨O-
               ⎝S-
```

```
GRA R6,2 C4,C1,C1,C1
```

The alternative atoms are each awarded a separate number, by entering C1 three times. At first they are shown as isolated atoms unconnected to the basic molecule.

```
           7
           C????C????C????C
           ?    8    9   10
           ?
      2    C
    1  ?   ?    3
    C?      ?  C
    ?          ?
    ?          ?
    C          C
  6   ?    ?   4
      ?  C?
      5
```

C 11   C 13

                          C 12

Atoms 11, 12 and 13 are then changed to N, O and S, and with the NSP RC entry they are defined either as part of a chain or a ring. Atom 10 is declared to be a variable group consisting of atoms 11, 12 and 13.

```
NOD 4 6 11 N,12 O,13 S,10 G1,NSP 11 12 13 RC,VAR
G1=11/12/13,BON ALL SE,DIS SIA
```

The additional command DIS SIA (Structure Images and Attributes) causes the following information to be displayed. The node specification (NSPEC) is evident:

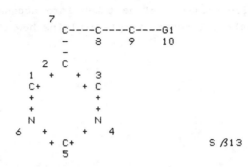

```
         7
         C----C----C----G1
         -    8    9    10
         -
     2   C
   1  +    +  3
   C+         + C
   +           +
   +           +
   N           N
 6   +    +  4
       + C+                        S ß13
       5
```

N ß11

O ß12

```
VAR G1=11/12/13
NODE ATTRIBUTES:
NSPEC    IS RC    AT  11
NSPEC    IS RC    AT  12
NSPEC    IS RC    AT  13

GRAPH ATTRIBUTES:
RING(S) ARE ISOLATED OR EMBEDDED
NUMBER OF NODES IS  13
```

RSP (Ring Specification)

If a structure in question contains rings or ring systems which can be "randomly substituted", this generally also includes fused rings. If the answers should be restricted to <u>substitutions</u> on the ring system, then the RSP entry is necessary. This specification then applies to all the rings in the structure. If substitution should be limited to only one ring then an atom number in this ring must be added, e.g. RSP 1 for the ring which contains atom number 1.

HCO (Hydrogen Count)

The HCO command saturates the free valences of the atoms in a structure with hydrogen. The H-count simply specifies whether substitutions or condensations are permissible or not at the open positions within a structure.

Example:

> R = any substituent, even H; no substitution
> in the ortho-position is permissible

The following H-counts must be entered:

At positions 2, 4 and 7 exactly 1 hydrogen atom   HCO 2 4 7 E1

On atom 10 a minimum of 2 hydrogen atoms   HCO 10 M2
(3 are also possible)

No H-count may be awarded to atoms 1, 5 and 6, as substitution is permissible at these positions. However, that does not mean that substitution necessarily occurs at these positions.

The H-count is integrated into the structural display:

Special Hints

Although the output formats may contain bibliographic data, abstract texts and index terms the output of the Registry File is intended for structure searches. The CA File is available for text searches. There are, however, a number of further search possibilities of which the following will be briefly described in this book:
1.   Searches with CAS Registry Numbers
2.   Searches with complete substance names (name match)
3.   Searches with substance names and name fragments
4.   Searches with molecular formulae
5.   Searches with chemical elements

It is important to point out that all online systems, including CAS ONLINE, are constantly undergoing further development. Thus, searches with "Markush formulae" are also possible in CAS ONLINE and it is no longer necessary to restrict substituents to one single atom. They can consist of certain specified functional groups.

Example:

$R = H, CH_3, CH_2-CH_3,$
$OH, NH_2, NHCH_3$

Furthermore, there are a series of additional refinements and improvements. However, they are outside the scope of this chapter which is intended to provide a basic introduction to the subject.

8.2.2 Searches with Structures

Enter the database:

        FILE REG

The confirmation message appears:

FILE "REGISTRY" ENTERED AT O9:3O:26 ON 27 APR 87
COPYRIGHT 1987 BY THE AMERICAN CHEMICAL SOCIETY

Sample search: Find pyrimidine derivatives with the following structural features

N = tertiary amine, also cyclic

R = -S-, -O-, -N<, but not
    -SH, -OH, -NH- or -NH$_2$

Hal = halogen

Terminal type 3 (non-graphic) is entered. The search can be carried
out on any kind of teletype terminal (printer or monitor screen terminal) and will produce results like those shown here.

A structure search is initiated with the symbols STR (=structure):

        STR

The system adds a colon (:) which indicates that structural entries
can be made.

        :GRA R6,DIS   The DIS command means the structure
                                   should be displayed. As in this case,
                                   it can be added to a structural in-
                                   put or entered separately immediate-
                                   ly after the colon.

```
            2
            C
  1     ?    ?    3
    C?      ? C
    ?          ?
    ?          ?
    C          C
  6    ?    ?    4
     ? C?
       5
```

The system numbers the atoms clockwise. The substituents can now be placed in the correct positions:

```
        :GRA 1 C1,3 C1,5 C1,2 C2,C1,C1,C1,DIS
```

```
                        10
                      C????C
                       ?     11
                       ?
        7  C         2 C          C 8
           ?   1  ?      ?  3 ?
          ?C?          ?  C?
           ?             ?
           ?             ?
           C             C
        6    ?  5  ?   4
             ?  C?
             ?
             ?
             C 9


C 12                                      C 14




                    C 13
```

Now the bonds must be specified. All the bonds are single with the exception of the ring, which is aromatic and has normalized bonds. The following entry is possible:

```
        :BON  ALL SE, R 1 2 N,DIS
```

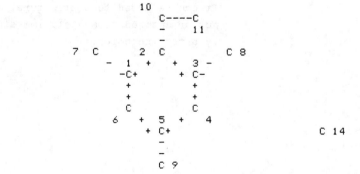

```
                        10
                      C----C
                       -    11
                       -
        7  C         2 C          C 8
           -   1  +      +  3 -
          -C+          +  C-
           +             +
           +             +
           C             C
        6    +  5  +   4
             +  C+
             -
             -
             C 9


C 12                                      C 14




                    C 13
```

R 1 2 N means the ring containing atoms 1 and 2 (it could equally well be 5 and 6) is normalized.

The bonds are now indicated by the symbols which were introduced at the beginning of this chapter (+ for normalized , - for single exact).

The next step is to specify the non-carbon atoms. In this example the carbon atoms at positions 4, 6 and 8 are replaced by nitrogen, 7 is a halogen. The alternative atoms N, O and S are assigned to the nodes 12 (N), 13 (O) and 14 (S). Position 9 bears the variable group G1.

```
:NOD 4 6 8 N,7 X,12 N,13 O,14 S,9 G1,VAR G1=12/13/14,DIS

                               10
                              C----C
                              -    11
                              -
               7  X       2  C              N 8
                      -  1  +    +  3  -
                     -C+           +  C-
                      +              +
                      +              +
                      N              N
                    6   +  5   +   4
      N β12                 +  C+                       S β14
                           -
                           -
                          G1  9



                            O β13
VAR G1=12/13/14
```

As no substitution is permissible at position 10, the two free valences must be saturated with hydrogen (hydrogen count E2). Positions 8, 11, 12, 13 and 14 can be substituted at random and can be either part of a ring or a chain. The latter is indicated by the node specification command NSP RC.

```
        :HCO 10 E2,NSP 8 11 12 13 14 RC
```

The END command indicates that the structure input is complete and the system assigns the number L1 to the structure.

```
        :END
        L1    STRUCTURE CREATED
```

A more detailed report about the input, which also includes the node
specification of the structure, can be recalled:

```
        DIS L1
```

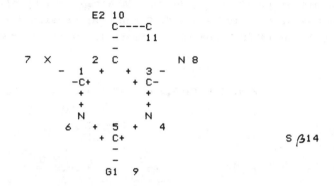

```
                            E2 10
                              C----C
                              -    11
                              -
        7   X       2   C              N 8
          -  1  +      +  3 -
          -C+           + C-
          +             +
          +             +
          N             N
        6   +   5   +   4
            + C+
            -
            -
        G1   9
```

N β12   S β14

```
                            O β 13
```

```
VAR G1=12/13/14
NODE ATTRIBUTES:
HCOUNT  IS E2     AT  10
NSPEC   IS RC     AT   8
NSPEC   IS RC     AT  11
NSPEC   IS RC     AT  12
NSPEC   IS RC     AT  13
NSPEC   IS RC     AT  14

GRAPH ATTRIBUTES:
RING(S) ARE ISOLATED OR EMBEDDED
NUMBER OF NODES IS  14
```

For the sake of comparison, here is the same structure displayed on a
graphics terminal (type 2):

Instead of creating a structure in several steps as we have shown here the commands can be stacked. However, it is essential to know the order in which the atoms, especially those in rings and ring systems, are numbered by the system. As already mentioned, this generally happens in a predictable sequence. It is advantageous, especially when microcomputers are used as terminals, to build up a structure "offline", i.e. before the link with the database is established.

In our example the entire input could be combined into one string - a stack - as follows:

```
GRA  R6,1 C1,3 C1,5 C1,2 C2,C1,C1,C1,BON ALL SE,R 1 2 N,
NOD 4 6 8 N,7 X,12 N,13 O,14 S,9 G1,VAR G1=12/13/14,
HCO 10 E2,NSP 8 11 12 13 14 RC
```

Now the search is initiated by:

```
S L1 SSS FUL
```

SSS means "substructure search". An inexpensive possibility of searching for certain precisely defined substances is offered, called EXACT (EXA) or FAMILY (FAM). FAMILY is used when so-called "dot-disconnected formulae", e.g. salts or polymers of certain precisely defined substances are to be included in the search. The FUL command means that the search is carried out in the entire file. It is also possible to carry out range searches (covering a specific range of Registry Numbers which can be freely selected) as well as sample searches. The latter is automatically carried out when no other option is specified;

in the present example the command S L1 is sufficient to initiate a sample search. It covers about 5 % of the whole file and is free of charge and serves as a means of testing a search strategy, e.g. to determine whether too many answers can be expected from searching the whole file or even if the maximum number of answers (5000) will be exceeded.

Shortly after the above command has been entered the following message appears:

SEARCH INITIATED (9:43:13)

The system does not automatically give any further information about the progress of the search. This must be requested by entering the command STA (status)

:STA

SEARCH EXECUTING

SEARCHED	SEARCH TIME	ANSWERS	PROJECTED ANSWERS
0.501 %	00.00.10	1	1 TO 797

The first answer was already found when only 0.5 % of the file had been searched. Based on this information the system gives a rather high estimate of the total number of expected answers, i.e. 797 structures.

:STA

SEARCH EXECUTING

SEARCHED	SEARCH TIME	ANSWERS	PROJECTED ANSWERS
30.233 %	00.01.56	1	1 TO 12

When approximately 30 % of the file has been covered the number of answers has not increased, thus the original estimate has been reduced to a total of 12 expected answers. After 62 % of the file has been searched 25 answers have been found and a total of 62 are expected:

```
:STA
```

```
SEARCH EXECUTING
SEARCHED          SEARCH TIME     ANSWERS      PROJECTED ANSWERS
62.521 %          00.03.43          25           25 TO     62
```

The search time can be utilized to view answers which have already
been found. After entering the number of the desired answer the structure diagram is displayed in the standard format. This standard format
(the default format) contains:

> CAS Registry Number (RN)
>
> Nomenclature (IN)
>
> Synonyms, a maximum of 50 (SY)
>
> Molecular formula (MF)
>
> Structure diagram
>
> Number of CA references, i.e. the number of publications in
> which this substance has been cited. If the CAOLD File
> contains publications about the substance this is in-
> dicated as follows:
>
> REFERENCES IN FILE CAOLD   (PRIOR TO 1967)

> :5   Answer number 5 is retrieved.

```
RN  23994-34-5                                                    ANS 5
IN  Pyrimidine,
    4-chloro-6-(dimethylamino)-5-(p-ethoxybenzyl)-2-(methylthio)- (8CI)
MF  C16 H20 Cl N3 O S
```

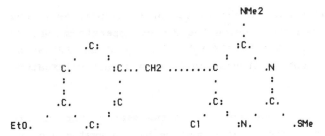

```
1 REFERENCES IN FILE CA (1967 TO DATE)
SEARCH EXECUTING -   33 ANSWERS
```

The same structure diagram as shown on a type 2 terminal:

The next status display finally announces the end of the search:

```
:STA
FULL FILE  SEARCH  COMPLETE
SEARCHED        SEARCH TIME      ANSWERS
100.000 %       00.05.56           39
```

Thirty nine answers were found, the search time – which depends, among other factors, on the number of simultaneous users – was 5.56 min.

The END command indicates that the search is finally completed. The answers are awarded the number L2:

```
:END
FULL FILE SEARCH COMPLETE
L2              39 SEA SSS FUL L1
```

It is also possible to link several structures or substructures to one query by means or their L-numbers using the Boolean operators AND, OR and/or NOT, e.g. S L1 OR L2 NOT L3 SSS FUL, whereby L1 and L2 can be alternative supplementary substructures and L3 is a structural feature to be excluded.

In addition, so-called screens can be used in the search. Screens are automatically generated from the input structure by the system and are used for a preselection prior to the actual (iterative) search. They can, however, be entered manually as additional requirements or restrictions which limit the number of answers in the search. Screens are numerical codes describing structural features. They are described in the "CAS ONLINE Screen Dictionary". The use of screens opens new possibilities for describing a structure or substructure in a search e.g.

the search for polymers. In the Registry File there is no other means of specifying that a substructure should be part of a macromolecular substance or that it should <u>not</u> be part of a polymer than by entering the appropriate Screen Number (2043 for "polymers general"). However, a detailed description of such refinements are outside the scope of this chapter.

8.2.3 Online Output of Search Results

Different output formats are available. The standard format SUB was already described in the course of the sample search. The literature references (CA abstract numbers) pertaining to the CAS Registry Numbers obtained from the search are requested by entering REG CAN, the structure diagram and the appropriate literature references are obtained by entering SUB CAN. The details included in these formats is normally sufficient when the printed version of Chemical Abstracts is available for further consultation. If this is not the case, it is advisable to select the SUB BIB format (giving the bibliographic data) or SUB BIB ABS (including the abstract, if available). However, only ten - the most recent - literature references (CA references) are cited from the Registry File. If there are more they can only be obtained by tranferring the CAS Registry Numbers "en bloc" (automatically) or singly (manually) to the CA File and carrying out a subsequent search in this file.

In this example answer 10 from answer set L2 should be displayed in format SUB BIB:

        D L2 10 SUB BIB

```
RN  24138-68-9                                                    ANS 10
IN  Pyrimidine,
    4-chloro-6-(diethylamino)-5-(p-ethoxybenzyl)-2-(methylthio)- (8CI)
MF  C18 H24 Cl N3 O S
```

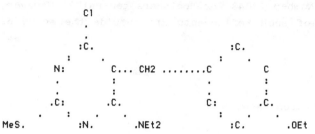

```
1 REFERENCES IN FILE CA (1967 TO DATE)

REFERENCE  1

AN  CA71(23):112877p
TI  Pyrimidine derivatives.  VII.  Monoamino- and monohydrazino
    derivatives of 2-methylthio-5-(p-alkoxybenzyl)chloropyrimidines
AU  Aroyan, A. A.; Kaldrikyan, M. A.; Grigoryan, L. A.
CS  Inst. Tonkoi Org. Khim.
LO  Erevan, USSR
SO  Arm. Khim. Zh., 22(5), 401-5
SC  28 (Heterocyclic Compounds (More Than One Hetero Atom))
DT  J
CO  AYKZAN
PY  1969
LA  Russ
```

It is not necessary to specify the answer set (in this case L2) if it
was the last set to be retrieved.

Now the answers 1-5 from L2 in the REG CAN format:

          D 1-5 REG CAN

```
RN  32672-48-3                                                   ANS 1
REFERENCES
1       CA74(15):76385c
RN  23994-31-2                                                   ANS 2
REFERENCES
1       CA71(23):112877p
RN  23994-32-3                                                   ANS 3
REFERENCES
1       CA71(23):112877p
RN  23994-33-4                                                   ANS 4
REFERENCES
1       CA71(23):112877p
RN  23994-34-5                                                   ANS 5
REFERENCES
1       CA71(23):112877p
```

Substances 2 to 5 are found in the same CA abstract (71:112877).

Besides the structure diagrams the format TRIAL supplies the CA nomenclature as well as the number of CA references. As neither the CAS
Registry Number nor the bibliographic data are shown, this format is
only useful for checking the structure diagram. This format is free of
charge.

          D 5 TRIAL

ANS 5
IN Pyrimidine,
    4-chloro-6-(dimethylamino)-5-(p-ethoxybenzyl)-2-(methylthio)- (8CI)

1 REFERENCES IN FILE CA (1967 TO DATE)

8.2.4 Offline Output of Search Results

The printout is initiated by the user at his terminal and the results
are sent to him by mail.

The commands are identical to those for the online output except that
the display command "D" is replaced by the print command "PRI". In
contrast to the online output, all answers are printed when no range
is specified. The formats are the same with the exception of TRIAL
which is inadmissible for an offline print.

        PRI SUB BIB
        L2 CONTAINS 39 ANSWERS CREATED ON 08 MAY 87 AT 06:24:48
        MAILING ADDRESS = H.R. ONLINER
                          HOECHST AG
                          WISS.DOK., F 821
                          D-6230 FRANKFURT/MAIN 80
                          WEST GERMANY

CHANGE MAILING ADDRESS? (N)/Y: N
39 ANSWERS PRINTED FOR REQUEST NUMBER P129084Q

No temporary change of mailing address is entered. All 39 answers from the last set of answers (in this case, L2) are printed in the format SUB BIB.

Here is an example of an offline printout:

STN™INTERNATIONAL

PRINT RESULTS - P129084Q   08 MAY 84 12:02:41   PAGE   3

REGISTRY NUMBER = 24138-68-9   ANSWER NUMBER = 1
INDEX NAME = Pyrimidine, 4-chloro-6-(diethylamino)-5-(*p*-ethoxybenzyl)-2-(methylthio)- (8CI)
MOLECULAR FORMULA = $C_{18}H_{24}ClN_3OS$

1 REFERENCES IN FILE CA (1967 TO DATE)
REFERENCE   1
AN   CA71(23):112877p
TI   Pyrimidine derivatives.   VII.   Monoamino- and monohydrazino derivatives of
      2-methylthio-5-(p-alkoxybenzyl)chloropyrimidines
AU   Aroyan, A. A.; Kaldrikyan, M. A.; Grigoryan, L. A.
CS   Inst. Tonkoi Org. Khim.
LO   Erevan, USSR
SO   Arm. Khim. Zh., 22(5), 401-5
SC   28 (Heterocyclic Compounds (More Than One Hetero Atom))
DT   J
CO   AYKZAN
PY   1969
LA   Russ

The results of a structure search in the Registry File are individual substances which are clearly identified by their CAS Registry Number. In many cases a search in the Registry File is sufficient to obtain all the information required. However, it is necessary to transfer the Registry Numbers to continue the search in the CA File whenever non-structural features have to be entered. The transfer is extremely simple with the CAS ONLINE system. It is described in 8.3.5 (Further Processing of the Results of a Structure Search).

8.2.5 Searches with CAS Registry Numbers

Apart from searches with structural input, structure diagrams and the reference data can also be retrieved from the Registry File by entering specific CAS Registry Numbers. This is, for instance, very convenient when a CAS Registry Number has been obtained as a result of a search in another file or by studying the literature. It can save the often time-consuming translation of the systematic name into a structure diagram. The CAS Registry Number is entered preceded by the DIS command (for an online output) or PRI (for an offline printout), but ACC (for accession number) must be placed either between the command and the Registry Number or following the latter. Up to 20 CAS Registry Numbers, separated by commas, can be stacked. The output is generated in the usual Registry File format:

DIS ACC 60538-42-3,191-48-0

or DIS 60538-42-3,191-48-0 ACC

RN   60538-42-3   ANS 1
IN   Hexaspiro[2.0.2.0.2.0.2.0.2.0.2.0]octadecane (9CI)
SY   [6]-Rotane
MF   C18 H24

5 REFERENCES IN FILE CA (1967 TO DATE)

RN   191-48-0   ANS 1
IN   Diacenaphtho[1,2-j:1',2'-l]fluoranthene (7CI, 8CI, 9CI)
SY   Decacyclene
DR   27581-78-8
MF   C36 H18
CI   COM, RPS, TSCA

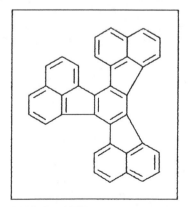

REFERENCES IN FILE CAOLD (PRIOR TO 1967)
63 REFERENCES IN FILE CA (1967 TO DATE)

8.2.6 Searches with Substance Names and Name Fragments

Substance Names

The search is initiated with the command S. The field identifier CN (complete name) must always be entered:

```
        S "JULIN'S CARBON CHLORIDE"/CN
        L1        1 "JULIN'S CARBON CHLORIDE"/CN
```

Because the name includes a word with an apostrophe (Julin's) the whole substance name (search term) must be written in inverted commas. If they are omitted an error message is received:

```
        S JULIN'S CARBON CHLORIDE/CN

        MISMATCHED QOUTE `JULIN'S'
```

When a character masking symbol (?) is used:

```
        S JULIN?/CN
        L2        2 JULIN?/CN
```

Two answers are received in this case. Besides `Julin's carbon chloride' there is a substance called `juline'.

Output of the result: D 1-2

```
RN  204-18-2
IN  3H,5H-Benzo[ij]quinolizine (8CI)
SY  Juline
MF  C12 H11 N
```

```
        : C.
       :       .
     C         C
     .         .
     .         .
   : C.       . N.
   :     .  .    .
 C       C       C
 .       :       .
 .       :       .
 C:     . C.    :C
   :   .    .  :
     C         C
```

0 REFERENCES IN FILE CA (1967 TO DATE)
```
RN  118-74-1
IN  Benzene, hexachloro- (8CI, 9CI)
SY  Bunt-cure
SY  Bunt-no-more
SY  Anticarie
SY  HCB
SY  Hexachlorobenzene
SY  Julin's carbon chloride
SY  No Bunt
SY  No Bunt 40
SY  No Bunt 80
SY  No Bunt Liquid
SY  Perchlorobenzene
SY  Sanocide
SY  Amatin
SY  Co-op Hexa
SY  Pentachlorophenyl chloride
SY  Snieciotox
MF  C6 Cl6
CI  COM, TSCA
```

```
              Cl
               .
 Cl            .
   .         .C:        .Cl
     .    .    :    .
       C         C
       :         .
       :         .
     . C.       :C.
       .    .  :    .
     .     C.        Cl
 Cl        .
           .
          Cl
```

REFERENCES IN FILE CAOLD (PRIOR TO 1967)
2141 REFERENCES IN FILE CA (1967 TO DATE)

Another example:

        S VITAMIN B12/CN

        L1   1 VITAMIN B12/CN

Abbreviated output of the answer:

        RN 68-19-9
        IN Vitamin B12 (8CI, 9CI)
        SY Anacobin
        SY Betalin-12
        SY Betaline-12
        SY Byladoce
        .

        .

        .

        etc, up to 50 synonyms

        REFERENCES IN FILE CAOLD (PRIOR TO 1967)
        4576 REFERENCES IN FILE CA (1967 TO DATE)

If the masked search term "Vitamin" is entered, all the vitamins are
found:

        S VITAMIN ?/CN
        L2   371 VITAMIN ?/CN

Name Fragments

The 12 million substance names at present stored in the Registry File
were split up into the smallest possible fragments (according to syl-
lables and punctuation) which are searchable in the Basic Index.
Example: 3,5-dichloro-2-methoxybenzoic acid was split up into

        3
        5
        di
        chloro
        2
        meth
        oxy
        benz
        oic
        acid

This means that, e.g. "methoxy" or "benzoic" are not searchable fragments. By using proximity operators the name fragments can be put into
the desired sequence (W is a proximity operator):

        S 3(W)5(W)DI(W)CHLORO(W)2(W)METH(W)OXY(W)BENZ(W)OIC(W)ACID

         3594302 3
         2323681 5
        32963873 DI
         1019251 CHLORO
         4668413 2
          794569 METH
         1589889 OXY
          395663 BENZ
          568673 OIC
         1828795 ACID

L3   2 3(W)5(W)DI(W)CHLORO(W)2(W)METH(W)OXY(W)BENZ(W)OIC(W)ACID

Two answers were found. Output of the results:

```
          D 1-2
RN   34165-26-9                                                      ANS 1
IN   Benzoic acid, 3,5-dichloro-2-methoxy-, hydrazide (9CI)
SY   3,5-Dichloro-2-methoxybenzoic acid hydrazide
MF   C8 H8 C12 N2 02

Cl
  .          :C.        .CONHNH2
       .      :    .   .
            C         C
            .          :
            .          :
            C:        .C.
             :    .     .
               C.          OMe
               .
               .
               Cl
2 REFERENCES IN FILE CA (1967 TO DATE)
RN   22775-37-7                                                      ANS 2
IN   Benzoic acid, 3,5-dichloro-2-methoxy- (9CI)
SY   o-Anisic acid, 3,5-dichloro- (7CI, 8CI)
SY   3,5-Dichloro-2-methoxybenzoic acid
SY   Salicyn (growth stimulant)
SY   2-Methoxy-3,5-dichlorobenzoic acid
MF   C8 H6 C12 03
CI   COM
             CO2H
             .
             C:        OMe
           .    :
         C.      :C.
         :        .
         :        .
         C         C
       .    .   :    .
    .      .C:      .Cl
Cl.
REFERENCES IN FILE CAOLD (PRIOR TO 1967)
12 REFERENCES IN FILE CA (1967 TO DATE)
```

Of course, it is not advisable to search with so many name fragments which must also be put into a certain sequence, as it takes quite a long time to obtain the result. Searches for individual substances are much more efficiently executed using the molecular formula with the addition of one or more unequivocal name fragments if necessary.

The Boolean operators AND, OR and NOT can also be used.

8.2.7 Searches with Molecular Formulae

The molecular formula can be used to search in the Basic Index without
a field descriptor or in the molecular formula field with the descriptor /MF. The atoms are entered according to the Hill System, i.e.
first carbon, then hydrogen followed by the remaining atoms in alphabetical order. All the elements are arranged alphabetically in substances which do not contain carbon. In the case of substances containing carbon, first the number of carbon atoms is mentioned then the
number of hydrogen atoms (if present) followed by all the other elements in alphabetical order.

Single component substances as well as multi-component substances
(dot-disconnected molecular formulae, e.g. copolymers or salts) are
retrieved from the Basic Index even if only one single component of a
multicomponent substance is sought.

        S C8H6CL2O3
        L12   724 C8H6CL2O3

A set of 724 answers (chemical substances) is retrieved, most of which
are multi-component substances, as shown by a comparable search in the
molecular formula field:

        S C8H6CL2O3/MF
        L13   95 C8H6CL2O3

"Only" 95 single component substances have the molecular formula
C8H6CL2O3.

The molecular formula field (/MF) consists of complete molecular formulae only. Multi-component substances are not automatically retrieved
with the individual components. They are only found in this field when
all the components are included in the search command:

        S C12H24N6.C8H6CL2O3/MF
        L15   1 C12H24N6.C8H6CL2O3/MF

Output of the results: D

RN 95555-81-0   ANS 1
IN Acetic acid, (2,4-dichlorophenoxy)-, compd. with
    N2,N4,N6-triisopropylmelamine (7CI)
MF C12 H24 N6 . C8 H6 C12 O3

        CM 1   Komponente 1

        RN 5465-03-2
        MF C12 H24 N6
        CI COM

i-PrNH
        .   . N: .NHPr-i
                     .   .   :   .
                    C   C
                    :   .
                    :   .
                    N.   N
                     .   :
                     C
                     .
                     NHPr-i

        CM 2   Komponente 2

        RN 94-75-7
        MF C8 H6 C12 O3
        CI COM

           C.   OCH2CO2H
          :   .   .
       C: .C.
        .   :
        .   :
        C   C
     .   .   .
        :C.   .Cl
Cl.

REFERENCES IN FILE CAOLD (PRIOR TO 1967)
0 REFERENCES IN FILE CA (1967 TO DATE)

8.2.8 Searches with Chemical Elements

Individual elements of a molecular formula can be used to search by
means of the "element count". The symbols for the elements are entered, as well as X for any halogen and M for any metal. The required
frequency of the elements is specified, followed by their symbols.

Requirements: Input:

exactly 3 atoms of iron in
the molecule   S 3/FE

3-7 fluoride atoms in
the molecule   S 3-7/F

more than 4 sulphur atoms
in the molecule   S S > 4

at least 1 magnesium atom
in the molecule   S MG > 0

not more than 3 phosphor atoms in
the molecule (but at least 1)   S P ⩽ 3

Explicit exclusion of elements from substances is only possible for C,
H, N and O and this is expressed as follows:

                                            S 0/C
                                            S 0/H
                                            S 0/N
                                            S 0/O

This kind of exclusion is only practicable in conjunction with another
requirement:

        S 12/C AND 26/X AND 0/H

Twelve carbon atoms and 26 random halogen atoms must be present, hydrogen is inadmissible. Other elements can be present.

Elements of a molecular formula are always counted as part of only one
component of a multicomponent substance:

        C2H4O2 . C4H11N   is counted as

        2/C   4/C
        4/H   11/H
        2/O   1/N

If element counts are linked with the AND operator, the result of the
following search:

    S 2/C AND 4/H AND 1/N

is the above mentioned multicomponent substance. If all the elements should be included in the same component they must be linked with the L-operator:

    S 8/C(L)4/N(L)1-3/S   answers include C8H8N4S2
                                        or C8H8N4S . C6H3N3O7

                                but not C8H8S . C6N4

as the required 4 nitrogen atoms are not contained in the same component as the C and H atoms.

8.3 Searching the CA File

Enter the database:

    FILE CA

The following confirmation message is shown:

    FILE "CA" ENTERED AT 03:21:39 ON 30 JAN 87
    COPYRIGHT 1987 BY THE AMERICAN CHEMICAL SOCIETY

The arrow ($\Rightarrow$) is the system prompt for input.

8.3.1 Searching in the Basic Index

The Basic Index contains   - Index Terms (IT)
                            - CAS Registry Numbers (RN)
                            - Titles
                            - Keywords (KW)

Masking symbol   ?

The subject of the search is "optical fibers from polymers, especially those made of polymethylmethacrylate". Each search is initiated by the command S:

```
     S OPTIC? AND FIBER?
            87596 OPTIC?
           119709 FIBER?
     L1      4648 OPTIC? AND FIBER?
```

4648 documents were found in which the two search terms were cited at least once in some context. The answer was awarded the number L1. (Please note that the American spelling: "fiber" is different from the British spelling: "fibre".)

The same problem is posed in context logic (proximity): the operator (W) (W = word) means "adjacent, in the order specified".

```
     S   OPTIC?(W)FIBER?

            87596 OPTIC?
           119709 FIBER?
     L2      2585 OPTIC?(W)FIBER?
```

In the reverse order:

```
     S   FIBER?(W)OPTIC?

           119709 FIBER?
            87596 OPTIC?
     L3      3791 FIBER?(W)OPTIC?
```

By combining the two sets of answers with the Boolean operator "OR" the total results are obtained:

```
     S L2 OR  L3

     L4   4000 L2 OR L3
```

A total of 4000 answers are retrievable.

The same result would have been obtained from the following entry:

```
S OPTIC?(W)FIBER? OR FIBER(W)OPTIC?
        87596 OPTIC?
       119709 FIBER?
         2585 OPTIC?(W)FIBER?
       119709 FIBER?
        87596 OPTIC?
         3791 FIBER?(W)OPTIC?
L5       4000 OPTIC?(W)FIBER? OR FIBER?(W)OPTIC?
```

In general, it is better to carry out searches using numerous search terms in several individual steps.

However, for situations like that shown above, CAS ONLINE offers a special solution, the operator (A) (A = adjacent). It stands for adjacent in any order:

```
S OPTIC?(A)FIBER?
```

```
        87596 OPTIC?
       119709 FIBER?
L6       4000 OPTIC?(A)FIBER?
```

The same 4000 answers are obtained in one step.

Now, however, glass fibers are not desired and all documents concerning glass fibers should be eliminated from the 4000 answers. This is achieved by using the Boolean operator "NOT" (Caution: documents containing phrases like e.g. "optical fibers made from glass or polymers" will also be excluded):

```
S L6 NOT GLASS
```

```
        93316  GLASS
L7       1915  L6 NOT GLASS
```

As shown the number of answers is reduced to less than half, from 4000 to 1915.

In order to make the search more precise only those documents, in which the search term "GLASS" is directly linked with "OPTICAL FIBER", should be excluded and not those in which it is mentioned in another context. This direct relationship is recognized by the Chemical Abstracts Service when these terms occur in the same index term field.

Example:

>   IT Glass fibers, preparation
>   (contg. germanium halide, for optical fibers)

The material (glass) and its properties or use (optical fibers) occur
in the same IT field. This condition is expressed using the operator
(L) (L = link) in CAS ONLINE.

>   S L6 NOT GLASS(L)OPTIC?(A)FIBER?

>   93316 GLASS
>   87596 OPTIC?
>   119709 FIBER?
>   1527 GLASS(L)OPTIC?(A)FIBER?
>   L8   2445 L6 NOT GLASS(L)OPTIC?(A)FIBER?

Compared to the L7 set of answers, about 500 less documents are now
excluded, among them, for example, one with the following IT fields:

>   IT Fiber, synthetic
>   (thermoplastic, for fiber optics)
>   IT Glass fibers, uses and miscellaneous
>   (fillers, for thermoplastic filaments)

The use of the (L) operator will be demonstrated again in another example a little later.

The number of anwers is definitely too high. Thus, answers should be
restricted to "fibers made of polymethylmethacrylate". The most effi-
cient way of achieving this is to enter the CAS Registry Number (RN),
which is 9011-14-7 for methylmethacrylate homopolymers (next section).

8.3.2 Searches with CAS Registry Numbers

As mentioned before the CAS Registry Numbers are contained in the
Basic Index in CAS ONLINE. Therefore, it is not necessary to enter a
field descriptor:

```
        S 9011-14-7 (RN for polymethylmethacrylate)

        L9  13796 9011-14-7
```

The answer is linked to L8 (from the last section):

```
        S L8 AND L9
```

54 answers. The same search in one step:

```
        S OPTIC?(A)FIBER? NOT GLASS(L)OPTIC?(A)FIBER?
          AND 9011-14-7

            87596 OPTIC?
           119709 FIBER?
             4000 OPTIC?(A)FIBER?
            93316 GLASS
            87596 OPTIC?
           119709 FIBER?
             1527 GLASS(L)OPTIC?(A)FIBER?
            13796 9011-14-7
        L11     54 OPTIC?(A)FIBER? NOT GLASS(L)OPTIC?(A)FIBER?
                   AND 9011-14-7
```

There are still 54 documents containing the required search terms in this case.

If a (P) (P = preparation) is added after the CAS Registry Number then only those documents describing the preparation of the substance with the appropriate RN will be selected.

```
        S  9011-14-7P

        L12    1886 9001-14-7P
```

Polymethylmethacrylate was cited 13796 times in some context (L9), but its preparation was only described 1886 times (L12).

Another example gives a better illustration of the usefulness of the proximity operator (L).

The subject of the search is: purification of vinyl chloride (RN 75-01-4):

        S 75-01-4

        L13   3316 75-01-4

        S L13 and PURIF?

            102667 PURIF?
        L14   108 L13 AND PURIF?

Vinyl chloride is cited 3316 times, in connection with the word frag-ment "PURIF?" 108 times. In this set of answers there are many which do not deal with the purification of vinyl chloride itself, but with the purification of other substances, e.g. the removal of vinyl chlo-ride.

Example: AN CA94(14):109006y
           TI Removing potential organic carcinogens and precursors
              from drinking water. Volume I Appendix A
           IT Water Purification
              (adsorption, of halogenated orgs. and trihalomethane
              precursors, from drinking water)
           IT 75-01-4
              (removal of, from drinking water by adsorption,
              evaluation of adsorbents for)

In all these cases the search terms 75-01-4 and PURIF? do not occur in the same IT field as the example shows. These can be eliminated as follows:

        S 75-01-4(L)PURIF?

        3316 75-01-4
        102667 PURIF?
        L15   40 75-01-4(L)PURIF?

Now 40 answers are found which are, for the most part, relevant:

        AN CA 83(22):179890d
        TI Purification of vinyl chloride
        IT 75-01-4P, preparation
                   (purifn. of, by distn.)

The RN for vinyl chloride and "purifn." occur in the same field.

8.3.3 Searches with Authors' Names

Publications written by J. Brandrup are sought. As authors' names are not part of the Basic Index, they must be accompanied by the field descriptor:

    S BRANDRUP, J?/AU

    L17   32 BRANDRUP; J?/AU

CA has registered 32 publications from J. Brandrup.

8.3.4 Searches with Corporate or Institute Names

The names of corporations or institutes are also not included in the Basic Index. The field descriptor CS (CS = corporate source) must be entered. Papers from the "Universitätsklinik Wien" (University Clinic, Vienna) about diabetes are sought:

    S UNIVERSITAETSKLIN?/CS

    L18   3453 UNIVERSITAETSKLIN?/CS

Now "Wien" (Vienna) must be entered, but the field descriptor LO (LO = location) must also be specified:

    S L18 AND VIENNA/LO

    12542 VIENNA/LO

    L19   390 L18 AND VIENNA/LO

And finally diabetes:

    S L19 AND DIABET?

```
        11854 DIABET?


L20     24 L19 AND DIABET?
```

Thus, 24 publications of the University Clinic, Vienna were found.

8.3.5 Further Processing of the Results of a Structure Search

The structure search in the Registry File (cf. 8.2, p. 150) generated
39 answers (= 39 chemical substances = 39 CAS Registry Numbers). The
final message was:

```
        FULL FILE SEARCH COMPLETE
        L2               39 SEA SSS FUL L1
```

These answers were temporarily filed under the number L2 and can be
subsequently displayed or further processed. The command:

```
        FILE CA
```

transfers the query to the CA File

```
        FILE "CA" ENTERED AT 09:31:13 ON 14 MAY 87
        COPYRIGHT 1987 BY THE AMERICAN CHEMICAL SOCIETY
```

When the appropriate literature references are sought the 39 CAS Registry Numbers contained in the L2 set of answers are interlinked with
"or". This is a simple command:

```
        S L2
        L3           4 L2
```

This shows that the 39 substances are all from 4 publications. This is
not unusual. On account of the specified substructure, they must certainly be similar substances with slightly different substituents, and
as such are often described as a group in scientific papers or patents.

As there are so few answers, there is no point in entering additional
search terms. The answers should be printed out and read through to
ascertain their relevance and enable further selection:

D1-4

ANSWER 1

```
AN  CA83(5):43369h
TI  Pyrimidine derivatives
AU  Narr, Berthold; Roch, Josef; Mueller, Erich; Haarmann, Walter
CS  Thomae, Dr. Karl, G.m.b.H.
LO  Ger.
PI  Ger. Offen. DE 2341925, 6 Mar 1975, 121 pp. Addn. to Ger. Offen.
    2,430,644.
AI  Appl. or Pr. P 23 41 925.2, 20 Aug 1973
CL  C07D, A61K
SC  28-17 (Heterocyclic Compounds (More Than One Hetero Atom))
DT  P
CO  GWXXBX
PY  1975
LA  Ger
```

ANSWER 2

```
AN  CA75(1):5830d
TI  Pyrimidine derivatives. XX. Substituted
    5-(p-allyloxybenzyl)pyrimidines
AU  Kaldrikyan, M. A.; Nersesyan, N. A.; Aroyan, A. A.
CS  Inst. Tonkoi Org. Khim.
LO  Erevan, USSR
SO  Arm. Khim. Zh., 24(1), 45-50
SC  28 (Heterocyclic Compounds (More Than One Hetero Atom))
DT  J
CO  AYKZAN
PY  1971
LA  Russ
```

ANSWER 3

```
AN  CA74(15):76385c
TI  Pyrimidine derivatives. XV. Reactions of 4,6-dichloro-,
    2-methylthio-4,6-dichloro-, and
    2,4,6-trihydroxy-5-(p-alkoxybenzyl)pyrimidines
AU  Kaldrikyan, M. A.; Grigoryan, L. A.; Aroyan, A. A.
CS  Inst. Tonkoi Org. Khim.
LO  Erevan, USSR
SO  Arm. Khim. Zh., 23(5), 462-8
SC  28 (Heterocyclic Compounds (More Than One Hetero Atom))
DT  J
CO  AYKZAN
PY  1970
LA  Russ
```

ANSWER 4

```
AN  CA71(23):112877p
TI  Pyrimidine derivatives. VII. Monoamino- and monohydrazino
    derivatives of 2-methylthio-5-(p-alkoxybenzyl)chloropyrimidines
AU  Aroyan, A. A.; Kaldrikyan, M. A.; Grigoryan, L. A.
CS  Inst. Tonkoi Org. Khim.
LO  Erevan, USSR
SO  Arm. Khim. Zh., 22(5), 401-5
SC  28 (Heterocyclic Compounds (More Than One Hetero Atom))
DT  J
CO  AYKZAN
PY  1969
LA  Russ
```

For demonstration purposes the answers are limited with the help of
the computer to German language publications:

```
S  L3 AND GER/LA
450729 GER/LA
L4              1 L3 AND  GER/LA
```

Only one publication remains, the one with GER (German) in the LA (=
language) field:

```
D CAN

CA83(5):43369h
```

In this way all the results of (sub-)structure searches can be matched
with any number of other search terms such as properties, uses, other
CAS Registry Numbers or CA Sections.

Transferring a search into the CAOLD File is an analogous procedure,
but, as mentioneed above, apart from the CAS Registry Number only the
document type "P" (patent) is searchable.

8.3.6 Online Output of Search Results

Online output means the output of search results on a monitor screen
or a printer. If the appropriate command "D" is used with no additional entry, then the first document of the most recently created set of
answers is displayed in the standard format. In the CA File of CAS
ONLINE the format BIB (BIB = bibliographic data) appears as follows:

ANSWER 1

```
AN   CA96(5):29024d
TI   Experience with a new adiuretin analog for the continuous
     therapy of diabetes insipidus in dogs
AU   Jaksch, Walter
CS   Med. Universitaetsklin., Veterinaermed. Univ.
LO   Vienna A-1090, Austria
SO   Wien. Tieraerztl. Monatsschr., 68(10), 344-55
SC   2-5 (Mammalian Hormones)
DT   J
CO   WTMOA3
IS   0043-535X
PY   1981
LA   Ger
```

The first document in the last answer set created (in this case L20 University Clinic, Vienna) is shown.

The first document of the answer set is retrieved with:

          D L17

ANSWER 1

```
AN   CA100(2):7442n
TI   Carboxylated fluoropolymers and fluorosulfate intermediates
AU   Blickle, Peter; Brandrup, Johannes; Millauer, Hans;
     Schwertfeger, Werner; Siegemund, Guenter
CS   Hoechst A.-G.
LO   Fed. Rep. Ger.
PI   Ger. Offen. DE 3230528 A1, 15 Sep 1983, 31 pp.
AI   Appl. 3230528, 17 Aug 1982; DE Appl. 3207142, 27 Feb 1982
CL   C08F14/18, C08F20/04, C08F214/26, C08F8/38, C08F8/12,
     C08J5/22, C25B13/08, C25B1/46
SC   35-8 (Chemistry of Synthetic High Polymers)
SX   38, 72
DT   P
CO   GWXXBX
PY   1983
LA   Ger
```

The fifth answer from L11 is retrieved using:

        D L11 5

ANSWER 5

AN   CA99(22):177109n
TI   Plastic optical fiber manufacture
CS   Nippon Telegraph and Telephone Public Corp.
LO   Japan
PI   Jpn. Kokai Tokkyo Koho JP 58/57101 A2 [83/57101], 5 Apr 1983,
     8 pp.
AI   Appl. 81/155506, 30 Sep 1981
CL   G02B5/14, G02B1/04-
SC   38-2 (Plastics Fabrication and Uses)
DT   P
CO   JKXXAF
PY   1983
LA   Japan

Further output formats:

Output of the first answer in the L4 set of answers in the above format plus CA abstract (ABS = abstract):

        D L4 BIB ABS

Output of the first 3 answers, then the fifth, and the seventh to
ninth answers of the last set in the standard format BIB:

        D 1-3,5,7-9

CA abstract numbers (= CAN) of documents 1-20 from the last set of answers:

        D 1-20 CAN

All the available information is obtained with the format "ALL". It
contains BIB, ABS and all the information in the fields IT and KW,
e.g. from the first three answers in set L15:

        D L15 1-3 ALL

The TRIAL format shows the fields TI, IT, KW and SC (CA Sections).
Retrieving this information is a good method of checking whether a
search has been effective, i.e. if the answers are relevant. As no CA
abstract numbers and no source references are given in this format, it
is free of charge.

```
    D   1-5 TRIAL
```

Finally, there is another free format (TI) which provides only the title of the document and the answer number. If required, a large number
of answers can be displayed with this command - this is somewhat
impractical with TRIAL because of the spacious texts - and their relevance can be roughly judged from the title.

```
    D L3 1-10 TI
```

In addition, a selective output of any desired field is possible (e.g.
D AN,TI).

8.3.7 Offline Output of Search Results

The printout is initiated from the user's terminal and the results are
sent to him by mail. It is only necessary to replace the display command "D" by the print command "PRI". The formats are identical to
those for online output with the exception of "TRIAL" and "TI" which
are impossible for offline printouts. In contrast to the "D" command,
all answers are printed if a certain range is not explicitly specified. The results are sent to the address which was given when the
user opened an account with STN. The system retrieves this address
every time a print command is entered and offers the possibility of
temporarily changing it. If this question is answered with "Y", another address with a maximum length of five lines can be entered and
it is valid for this particular printout. In the following example
this option has not been chosen and the question is answered with "N".

```
PRI

L20 CONTAINS 24 ANSWERS CREATED ON 31 JAN  86 AT
03:37:36
MAILING ADDRESS = H.R. ONLINER
                  MED. UNIVERSITAETSKLIN.
                  VETERINÄRMED. UNIV.
                  A-1090 VIENNA
                  AUSTRIA
CHANGE MAILING  ADDRESS (N)/Y:  N
24 ANSWERS PRINTED FOR REQUEST NUMBER P047018G
```

All the results in the last set of answers (L20) are printed in "BIB"
format.

As in the display command it is possible to select individual fields
in any combination using the print command.

8.4 Searching the CAOLD File

Enter the database:

```
CAOLD FILE
```

The confirmatory message appears:

```
FILE "CAOLD"  ENTERED AT 09:30:47 ON 10 APR 87
COPYRIGHT 1987 BY THE AMERICAN CHEMICAL SOCIETY
```


8.4.1 Searches with CAS Registry Numbers

The CAS Registry Numbers are in the Basic Index and no field specification is required.

```
S 110-86-1       (110-86-1 for pyridine)

L1    11 110-86-1
```

Eleven references are found. Entry of P in the DT (= document type) limits the answers to patents:

```
        S  L1 AND P/DT
        13918P/DT
        L2    1 L1 AND P/DT
```

Only 1 patent is among the 11 publications.

The same search in one step:

```
        S  110-86-1 AND P/DT

        11   110-86-1
        13918 P/DT


        L3    1 110-86-1 AND P/DT
```

This exhausts all the possibilities of searching in the CAOLD File.

8.4.2 Online Output of Search Results

CAOLD offers only 2 output formats: ALL   default
                                      CAN   CA abstract number (AN)
                                              and document type (DT),
                                              in the case of a patent
                                      TRIAL   CAS Registry Numbers
                                              only (IT)

D

ANSWER 1

AN CA65;16505c
DT P
IT 62-53-3   96-50-4 100-61-8   110-72-5 110-86-1
      111-40-0 111-42-2 122-39-4 141-43-5 462-08-8
      537-65-5 624-78-2 626-03-9 636-16-4 689-98-5
      1126-34-7 2457-47-8 2770-75-4 3088-27-5
      3400-38-2 6237-86-1 13725-36-5 13725-38-7
      13725-40-1 13725-42-3 13725-43-4 14650-46-5
      33776-96-4 84719-31-3

The output consists of the first (and in this case only) document of
the answer set L3 in the ALL format.

      D L1 1-5 CAN

      AN CA65:16505c
      AN CA65:12023h
      AN CA65:2108c
      AN CA65:2103c
      AN CA65:187b

Documents 1-5 of answer set L1 are shown in format CAN.

8.4.3 Offline Output of Search Results

Instead of "D" (for display) "PRI" (for print) is entered, e.g.

        PRI L11-5 CAN

The process is identical to that described for the CA File.

8.5 Logoff Procedure

When the search is complete the link to the host computer is disconnected with the following command:

LOG Y

CAS ONLINE confirms the command with

CAS ONLINE LOGOFF AT 03:38:51 ON 30 JAN 87

8.6 Charges for Using the Databases (January 1987)

The prices quoted here are standard prices. There is a 10 % to 30 % reduction for Chemical Abstracts subscribers.

Database	Costs of Usage per hour	Costs of Print-out (online)	Costs of Document (offline)
HOME file	$25.00		
CA File	$106.00	$0.09 - 0.93	$0.11 - 1.04
		depending on the format	
CAOLD File	$106.00	$0.11	$0.22
Registry File	$ 67.00	$0.09 -1.25	$0.11 - 1.36
(see below)		depending on the format	

The pricing for the Registry File is much more complicated than for the CA and CAOLD Files. In addition to the costs for the session time (charged per hour), search fees are also charged for each search. They total:

$99.00	for a "Full File Substructure Search" (SSS FUL)
$20.00	for EXACT or FAMILY searches (EXA FUL or FAM FUL with fully specified structures)
$10.50	for a Registry Number Range Search when only one range, e.g. the latest part of the file is to be searched and the number of the Registry Numbers contained in this range does not exceed 80,000
$ 0.63	for text searches (initiated with "S") per search term

It should also be noted that there is a special price for universities (academic programme): if they subscribe to Chemical Abstracts, universities pay only 10% of the standard price. For more information contact STN.

8.7 Example from the Registry File

```
RN   78945-33-2                                                      ANS 1
IN   Benzene, 1-(1-ethyl-1-methylhexyl)-3,5-dimethoxy- (9CI)
MF   C17 H28 O2
```

```
Typ-3-Terminal:                        Typ-2-Terminal (1024x780 Bildpunkte):
---------------                        -------------------------------------

                    Me
                     .
                     .
MeO.        .C:    .C(CH2)4Me
    .   .     :   .   .
      C       C
      :       .   Et
      :       .
      C.       :C
       .   :
         C
          .
          .
         OMe
```

1 REFERENCES IN FILE CA (1967 TO DATE)

REFERENCE   1

```
AN   CA95(13):114957j
TI   A new synthesis of 5-(1',1',1'-trialkylmethyl)resorcinols
AU   Singh, Vishwakarma; Kane, Vinayak V.; Martin, Arnold R.
CS   Coll. Pharm., Univ. Arizona
LO   Tucson, AZ 85721, USA
SO   Synth. Commun., 11(6), 429-37
SC   25-10 (Noncondensed Aromatic Compounds)
DT   J
CO   SYNCAV
IS   0039-7911
PY   1981
LA   Eng
AB   Alkanoylresorcinol ethers I (R = 1-hexyl, 1-pentyl) were converted to
     the title compds. II (R same as above; R1 = Me, Et, allyl; R2 = H)
     via the resp. III and II (R2 = Me).  The Wittig reaction of I (R =
     1-hexyl) with (EtO)2P(O)CH2N:CHPh and subsequent alkylation with MeI
     gave III (R = 1-hexyl, R1 = Me), the latter was reduced
     (Wolff-Kishner), and the II (R = 1-hexyl, R1 = R2 = Me) obtained was
     treated with Me3SiI to give II (R = 1-hexyl, R1 = Me, R2 = H).  For
     diagram(s), see printed CA Issue.
KW   resorcinol tertiary alkyl; alkylresorcinol tertiary;
     alkanoylresorcinol Wittig aminomethanephosphate
IT   39192-51-3   41497-32-9
        (Wittig reaction of, with [(benzylideneamino)methane]phosphonate
        diester, alkylation of product from)
IT   50917-73-2
        (Wittig reaction of, with dimethoxyphenyl alkyl ketones, and
        alkylation of products from)
IT   61133-09-3P   78945-37-6P   78945-38-7P   78945-39-8P   78945-40-1P
     78945-41-2P
        (prepn. and Wolff-Kishner redn. of)
IT   60526-81-0P   78945-32-1P   78945-33-2P   78945-34-3P   78945-35-4P
     78945-36-5P
        (prepn. and hydrolysis of, resorcinol analog from)
IT   56469-10-4P   78945-27-4P   78945-28-5P   78945-29-6P   78945-30-9P
     78945-31-0P
        (prepn. of)
```

8.8 Example from the CA File: Journal

AN CA83(22):180885n
TI Various transmission properties and launching techniques of plastic
    optical fibers suitable for transmission of high optical powers
AU Reidenbach, H. D.; Bodem, F.
CS Dep. Eng., Univ. Erlangen-Nuernberg
LO Erlangen, Ger.
SO Opt. Quantum Electron., 7(5), 355-60
SC 39-4 (Textiles)
SX 73
DT J
CO OQELDI
PY 1975
LA Eng
AB The output power of a composite fiber of .apprx.1.5 mm diam. with a
    core of polystyrene [9003-53-6] and a sheath of poly(methyl
    methacrylate) [9011-14-7] was measured as a function of the angle of
    incidence with the results interpreted using the ray optical fiber
    transmission model. Various launch-loss-reducing optical end-face
    working procedures were compared and a method to avoid Fresnel
    reflection losses by Brewster angled fiber input end-face for
    linearly polarized light beams was investigated. The transverse and
    longitudinal intensity distribution of the output beam of the fiber
    was measured.
KW plastic optical fiber transmission; synthetic optical fiber;
    polystyrene optical fiber; polymethyl methacrylate optical fiber
IT Synthetic fibers
        (methyl methacrylate-styrene, sheath-core composite, optical
        properties of)
IT Fiber optics
        (poly(methyl methacrylate)-polystyrene sheath-core composite
        fibers, transmission operatives of)
IT 9003-53-6
        (fiber, core, with poly(methyl methacrylate) sheath, optical
        properties of)
IT 9011-14-7
        (fiber, sheath, with polystyrene core, optical properties of)

8.9 Example from the CA File: Patent

AN   CA99(22):177109n
TI   Plastic optical fiber manufacture
CS   Nippon Telegraph and Telephone Public Corp.
LO   Japan
PI   Jpn. Kokai Tokkyo Koho JP 58/57101 A2 [83/57101], 5 Apr 1983, 8 pp.
AI   Appl. 81/155506, 30 Sep 1981
CL   G02B5/14, G02B1/04
SC   38-2 (Plastics Fabrication and Uses)
DT   P
CO   JKXXAF
PY   1983
LA   Japan
AB   A plastic (e.g., poly(Me methacrylate) (I) [9011-14-7] optical fiber
     with low transmitting light loss, comparable with that of an optical
     glass fiber, is produced by (1) purifying monomer(s), (2) mixing of
     the monomer(s), a polymn. initiator, and a chain transfer agent, (3)
     a polymn. of the mixt., (4) extruding the polymer (e.g., by
     extrusion) to give a core material, and (5) covering (e.g., by
     coextrusion) the core with a polymer (n less than that of the core),
     where 1-4 are done in a closed system at a reduced pressure. Thus, a
     mixt. (contg. dust particles .1toreq.1./cm3) of Me methacrylate,
     azo-tert-butane [927-83-3], and butyl mercaptan [109-79-5] was
     prepd at 150-200 mm-pressure, heated 16 h at 130.degree., and
     gradually heated to 180.degree. to give a I core material. A 25:75
     (molar) 2,2,3,3-tetrafluoropropyl
     methacrylate-2,2,3,3,4,4,5,5,-octafluorpentyl methacrylate copolymer
     (II) [87608-51-3] and the I were coextruded to give an optical fiber
     with core diam. 0.60 mm and II sheath thickness 0.10 mm. The optical
     fiber had transmitting light loss at 566 (516) nm at 62 (65)
     d.beta./km and almost no loss at .1toreq.5.80 nm due to micro air
     bubbles and dusts.
KW   polymethyl methacrylate optical fiber; fluoroalkyl methacrylate
     copolymer optical fiber; azobutane polymn initiator methyl
     methacrylate; butyl mercaptan chain transfer methacrylate
IT   Fiber optics
         (communication, low-mol.-wt. alkyl methacrylate polymer
         core-fluoroalkyl methacrylate copolymer sheath fibers for)
IT   Synthetic fibers
         (low-mol.-wt. alkyl methacrylate polymer core-fluoropolymer
         sheath, for communication optical fibers)
IT   87608-50-2   87608-51-3
         (alkyl methacrylate polymer core fibers covered with, for
         communication optical fibers)
IT   927-83-3
         (catalysts, for polymn. of low-mol.-wt. alkyl methacrylates for
         cores for communication optical fibers)
IT   109-79-5
         (chain transfer agents, in polymn. of low-mol.-wt. alkyl
         methacrylates for core materials for communication optical fibers)
IT   9010-87-1   9011-14-7
         (communication optical fibers, covered with fluoroalkyl
         methacrylate copolymers)

8.10 Example from the CAOLD File


```
AN  CA65:16505c
DT  P
IT  62-53-3   96-50-4   100-61-8   110-72-5   110-86-1   111-40-0
    111-42-2   122-39-4   141-43-5   462-08-8   537-65-5
    624-78-2   626-03-9   636-73-7   638-16-4   689-98-5   1126-34-7
    2457-47-8   2770-75-4   3088-27-5   3400-38-2   6237-86-1
    13725-36-5   13725-38-7   13725-40-1   13725-42-3   13725-43-4   14650-46-5
    33776-96-4   84719-31-3
```

```
* * * * * * * * * *    Welcome to STN International  * * * * * * * * * * *

                      New STN Features Now Available

                         Enter NEWS for Details

* * * * * * * * * * * * * * * * * * * * * * * * * * * * * * * * * * * * * *
FILE 'HOME' ENTERED AT 05:32:26 ON 23 OCT 84
```

① =>news ca

```
NEWS CA    Oct 14   Recent updates to the CA File

Recent Updates   Volume-Issue Pair

Oct 14, 1984    101-15/VI    101-16/VI
Sep 30, 1984    101-13/VI    101-14/VI
Sep 16, 1984    101-11/VI    101-12/VI
Sep  2, 1984    101- 9/VI    101-10/VI

The CA file contains 6,552,612 citations.  References are current
through Volume 101, Issue 16.  The CA file is updated biweekly.
```

② => news caold

```
NEWS CAO   Oct 21   Recent Updates to the CAOLD File

The CAOLD file contains records for documents covered in printed
Chemical Abstracts prior to 1967 which cite chemical substances that
are part of the Registry file.  The CAOLD file is being expanded incre-
mentally as the pre-1965 substances are added to the CAS Registry file.
Currently, the file contains  1;149,006 CA Reference Numbers.
The CAOLD file is updated weekly.
```

③ => news reg

```
NEWS REG    Oct 21   Recent updates to the Registry File

Recent Updates  Highest Registry Number

Oct 21, 1984    92691-26-4
Oct 14, 1984    92541-24-7
Oct  7, 1984    92418-10-5
Sep 30, 1984    92281-88-4

The Registry file contains 6,892,473 Registry Numbers.  All can be
displayed.  6,559,776 substances are searchable by structure.
The Registry file is updated weekly.  References are current through
Volume 101, Issue 16.
```

Fig. 89: Extract from STN International

9 Online Searches compared with Manual Searches

In order to clearly demonstrate the differences - advantages and dis-
advantages - between a literature search in print (Chemical Abstracts)
and an online search (CAS ONLINE), certain search problems from Chapter 2 will be repeated as an online search.

9.1 Sample search: Does CA Vol.98 contain abstracts about the Fischer
                  Tropsch synthesis? (cf. p. 57)
     To illustrate: CA File

After a link has been established with the host through the communication network, in this case via STN International (Fig. 89), the latest
information about the individual files can be recalled.

Explanation of Fig.89:
1. The arrow is a prompt which appears at the position on the screen
   where a search command should be entered. The most recent entries
   in the CA File are retrieved at "news ca": the latest information
   was updated on October 14th, 1984, in this case the contents of
   Chemical Abstracts issue nos. 15 and 16 of Vol. 101.
2. The CAOLD File, which is expanded every week, contained 1 149 006
   references to CA abstract numbers on October 21st, 1984.
3. The Registry File shows the most recent substance updates. The
   highest Registry Number on October 21st, 1984 was: 92691-26-4. At
   that time the Registry File contained 6 892 473 Registry Numbers.

The search for publications about the Fischer Tropsch synthesis is
carried out in the CA File (Fig. 90). In contrast to the search in the
printed version of Chemical Abstracts, "Fischer Tropsch" can be used
as a search term.

```
(1)-=> file ca
     FILE 'CA' ENTERED AT 05:33:35 ON 23 OCT 84
     COPYRIGHT 1984 BY THE AMERICAN CHEMICAL SOCIETY

(2)   =>  s fischer (w) tropsch range=(v98,v98)
(3)          ————110 FISCHER
(4)          ————71 TROPSCH
(5)-L1         71 FISCHER (W) TROPSCH

(6)———=> d bib ind

(7)-ANSWER 1

(8)———AN   CA98(26):222536s
(9)-TI    Modification of iron species in FeNaY zeolite by sodium chloride
          treatment
(10)——AU   Novakova, J.; Kubelkova, L.; Dolejsek, Z.; Wichterlova, B.; Kolihova,
          D.; Andera, V.
(11)-CS    J. Heyrovsky Inst. Phys. Chem. Electrochem.
(12)—LO    Prague 121 38, Czech.
(13)-SO    React. Kinet. Catal. Lett., 21(3), 273-6
(14)——SC   67-1 (Catalysis, Reaction Kinetics, and Inorganic Reaction Mechanisms
          )
(15)-DT    J
(16)-CO    RKCLAU
(17)-IS    0304-4122
(18)-PY    1982
(19)-LA    Eng
(20)-KW    iron zeolite catalyst Fischer Tropsch; sodium chloride treatment
          zeolite catalyst; redn iron zeolite catalyst pretreatment
(21)-IT    Hydrogenation catalysts
             (iron-contg. zeolites, sodium chloride treatment effect on)
     IT    Reduction
             (of iron-contg. zeolite catalysts, sodium chloride pretreatment
             effect on)
     IT    Zeolites, uses and miscellaneous
             (FeNaY, catalysts, for Fischer-Tropsch synthesis, sodium chloride
             treatment effect on)
     IT    7439-89-6, uses and miscellaneous
             (catalysts, zeolites contg., for Fischer-Tropsch synthesis, sodium
             chloride treatment effect on)
     TT    7647-14-5, uses and miscellaneous
             (iron-contg. zeolite catalysts treated with)
```

Fig. 90: Online search in the CA File

Explanation of Fig. 90:

1. The CA File is entered.
2. "s" denotes the search command: both "Fischer" and "Tropsch" should be sought, but only on condition that the words are immediately adjacent to each other. This is indicated by the proximity operator (w). The period to be searched is entered beside the term "range". In this case only Vol. 98 should be consulted (the start and end of the period must be defined). The period can refer to a particular CA issue, a certain year or several years.
3. "Fischer" was mentioned 110 times in the titles of abstracts, and/or the entries in the General Subject Index and/or the text modifications.
4. "Tropsch" was found 71 times.
5. The answer is stored under L1. The system automatically assigns a L (= line) number to each answer which is readily retrievable at any time for further searches or linking data.
6. The answers can be recalled and displayed on the screen by entering d (= display). The addition of "bib ind" signifies that the bibliographic information (bib) and the index entries (ind = index) should be shown for each answer.
7. Answer 1 is shown in this example.
8. AN = abstract number: CA volume, issue and abstract numbers
9. TI = title: title of the abstract
10. AU = author: name of the author
11. CS = corporate source: author's place of work
12. LO = location: address of the author's place of work
13. SO = source: title of the journal, vol. and issue number, number of pages
14. SC = section code: CA Section Number and the title of the section
15. DT = document type: form of the original publication, in this case J = journal
16. CO = CODEN
17. IS = ISSN
18. PY = publication year
19. LA = language of the publication
20. KW = keyword: entries from the Keyword Index of the CA issue
21. IT = index terms: entries from the CA volume indexes, first the terms from the controlled vocabulary and - instead of the CA Index Name - the CAS Registry Numbers, text modifications follow in brackets. Since June 1987 common names, generally those used by the author in the original publication, have been added to the Registry Numbers in the CA File. However, not all Registry Numbers can be identified in this way.

```
          => set range=(v98,v98)
          SET COMMAND COMPLETED

  (1)—— => s hydrogenation (1) carbon (w) monoxide
                     1601 HYDROGENATION
                     8193 CARBON
                     1275 MONOXIDE
  (2)—L2             140 HYDROGENATION (L) CARBON (W) MONOXIDE

  (3)—— => s heat of hydrogenation/cv
          L3            3 HEAT OF HYDROGENATION/CV

  (4)—— => s hydrogenation catalysts/cv
          L4          519 HYDROGENATION CATALYSTS/CV

  (5)—— => s kinetics of hydrogenation/cv
          L5           80 KINETICS OF HYDROGENATION/CV

  (6)—— => s methanation/cv
          L6           21 METHANATION/CV

  (7)—— => s heat of methanation/cv
          L7            3 HEAT OF METHANATION/CV

  (8)—— => s kinetics of methanation/cv
          L8            5 KINETICS OF METHANATION/CV

  (9)—— => s methanation catalysts/cv
          L9           44 METHANATION CATALYSTS/CV

 (10)—— => s fuel gas manufacturing/cv
          L10         277 FUEL GAS MANUFACTURING/CV

 (11)—— => s 12 or 13 or 14 or 15 or 16 or 17 or 18 or 19 or 110
          L11         889 L2 OR L3 OR L4 OR L5 OR L6 OR L7 OR L8 OR L9 OR L10

 (12)—— => s 111 not 11
          L12         824 L11 NOT L1

          => d bib ind

 (13)——ANSWER 1

          AN   CA98(26):223500n
          TI   Synfuels from fusion:  using the tandem mirror reactor and a
               thermochemical cycle to produce hydrogen
          AU   Werner, R. W.
          CS   Lawrence Livermore Natl. Lab.
          LO   Livermore, CA, USA
          SO   Report, UCID-19609; Order No. DE83005216, 546 pp.  Avail. NTIS
               From: Energy Res. Abstr. 1983, 8(7), Abstr. No. 14205
          SC   71-2 (Nuclear Technology)
          SX   51
          DT   T
          PY   1982
          LA   Eng
          KW   synthetic fuel hydrogen fusion reactor; tandem mirror reactor
               hydrogen prodn
          IT   Fuel gas manufacturing
                   (hydrogen, in nuclear mirror fusion reactor)
          IT   Nuclear fusion reactors
                   (mirror, hydrogen synthetic fuel prodn. in)
          IT   1333-74-0P, preparation
                   (manuf. of, in nuclear fusion reactor)
```

Fig. 91: Online search in the CA File

Seventy-one abstracts can be found for the term "Fischer Tropsch" alone. This term cannot be used in a search in the printed version of Chemical Abstracts. In addition, the terms which were used in the manual literature search (cf. p. 59) can also be entered in an online search. These terms must be found with the help of the Index Guide, as in a manual search. The online search with systematic terms is shown in Fig. 91.

Explanation of Fig. 91:
1. Search term: hydrogenation of carbon monoxide: the proximity operator (l=link) means that "hydrogenation" and "carbon monoxide" should be found in the same information unit e.g. title or keyword entries, or index entry together with the appropriate text modification. (w) specifies that the "carbon" and "monoxide" must be immediately adjacent to each other.
2. The answer is stored under L2: the specified search term combination is present 140 times in Volume 98.
3. - 10. The search terms obtained from the Index Guide are typed in individually. The addition of "cv" denotes that they are from the controlled vocabulary. For each search term the number of answers is shown and stored under L3 to L10.
11. The answers L2 to L10 are interlinked with the Boolean operator "OR" to eliminate possible duplicate results. A total of 889 citations are stored under L11.
12. In order to ascertain whether more abstracts containing the term "Fischer Tropsch" were found using the controlled vocabulary than with the term "Fischer Tropsch" alone, the number of abstracts contained under L11 which are not included in L1 should be shown. There are 824 abstracts, which means that six documents contain the term "Fischer Tropsch", but none of the terms from the controlled vocabulary. Thus, these were not found in the manual search.
13. Answer 1 of the 824 abstracts: this answer is not really relevant to the search problem. This clearly shows that each answer must be read through, as a lot of irrelevant information must be expected in 824 answers within one CA volume.

```
=> file reg
FILE 'REGISTRY' ENTERED AT 05:49:42 ON 23 OCT 84
COPYRIGHT 1984 BY THE AMERICAN CHEMICAL SOCIETY

=> match dos
L13            1 MAT DOS

=> d sub can
RN   122-62-3                                                    ANS 1
IN   Decanedioic acid, bis(2-ethylhexyl) ester (9CI)
MN   DOS
SY   PX 438
SY   Bis(2-ethylhexyl) sebacate
SY   Bisoflex DOS
SY   DOS
SY   Monoplex DOS
SY   Octoil S
SY   Staflex DOS
SY   Sebacic acid, bis(2-ethylhexyl) ester (8CI)
SY   Dioctyl sebacate
SY   Plexol
SY   Bisoflex
SY   Bis(2-ethylhexyl) decanedioate
SY   Plexol 201J
SY   Di-(2-Ethylhexyl)-sebacate
SY   Edenol 888
SY   Ergoplast SDO
SY   Sebacic acid di(2-ethylhexyl) ester
SY   Plasthall DOS
```

(continued overleaf)

Fig. 92: Online search in the Registry File and in the CA File

9.2 Sample Search: What was published about the plasticizer DOS in
Volume 98 of Chemical Abtracts?
    To illustrate: Registry File
                 CA File

It is not advisable to use the term "DOS" to search in the CA File, as
DOS is an acronym and it is unlikely that every author used this term.
The most reliable way of finding all the documents relating to DOS is
to use the Registry Number for the search, a possibility which is not
offered by the printed services. Using the systematic CA Index Name
for the online search is impossible because no CA Index Names are
stored in the CA File. If a substance name is known the Registry File
must first be consulted and then the search can be continued in the CA
File with the CAS Registry Number. Thus, compared to the search procedure in the printed version of Chemical Abstracts, an additional
step is necessary.

As shown in Fig. 92, the CAS Registry Number is first obtained from
the Registry File.

Explanation of Fig. 92:

1. Enter the Registry File
2. The "match" command links the entry to a precisely defined substance in the Registry File. The answer is recorded under L13.
3. All the information relevant to this substance is recalled with
   the "sub" (= substance) command. In addition, the CA abstract
   numbers should be listed (with the command "can" = CA number).
4. RN = CAS Registry Number
5. IN = systematic CA Index Name and also the collective period from
   which the name has been valid, in this case since 9CI, i.e. 1972,
   the beginning of the ninth collective period.
6. MN = match name: the search term which led to this information.
7. SY = synonyms: list of all trivial names, trade names and semi-
   systematic substance names which the Chemical Abstracts Service
   has found for this substance in the literature up to the present,
   in this case 18 different synonyms. A maximum of 50 synonyms are
   displayed on the screen.

(8)—MF   C26 H50 O4
(9)—CI   COM, TSCA;
(10)—DR   28986-40-5;

(11)————Me(CH2)3CHEtCH2OC(O)(CH2)8C(O)OCH2CHEt(CH2)3Me

(12)————REFERENCES IN FILE CAOLD (PRIOR TO 1967)
(13)—492 REFERENCES IN FILE CA (1967 TO DATE)
(14)——1   CA101(16):139260g
      2   CA101(16):131679e
      3   CA101(14):112748k
      4   P CA101(12):96243j
      5   CA101(10):73403x
      6   CA101(9):67550b
      7   CA101(8):57391m
      8   CA101(8):57382j
      9   CA101(8):55927s
      10   CA101(6):39624k

(15)————=) file ca
      FILE 'CA' ENTERED AT 05:50:51 ON 23 OCT 84
      COPYRIGHT 1984 BY THE AMERICAN CHEMICAL SOCIETY

(16)————=) s l13 range=(v98,v98)
      L14   17 L13

(17)————=) s dos range=(v98,v98)
      L15   5 DOS

(18)————=) s l14 or l15
      L16   22 L14 OR L15

                              (continued overleaf)

Continuation of Fig. 92

8. MF = molecular formula

9. CI = class identifier: states the class of compound to which the
   substance belongs, e.g. a mineral, a polymer, a radical or some
   other class, and whether the substance falls under the Toxic
   Substance Control Act (TSCA).

10. DR = deleted Registry Number: a CAS Registry Number which is no
    longer valid for this substance. It is advisable to carry out an
    additional search using deleted Registry Numbers, as some ab-
    stracts could be cited under them.

11. The structural formula of the substance as shown on a very simple
    terminal with no facility for graphic display.

12. Number of abstracts about DOS included in the CAOLD File, i.e. be-
    fore 1967. In this case there are none.

13. Number of abstracts about the substance DOS contained in the CA
    File. Since 1967 there have been 492 references to DOS.

14. List of numbers of the ten latest abstracts mentioning DOS. Ab-
    stracts dealing with patents are marked with the letter P (cf. Ab-
    stract no. 4).

15. "file ca" is entered at the next prompt to transfer from the Reg-
    istry File to the CA File.

16. The CAS Registry Number, recorded in L13, is used for the search
    in the CA File. The L-number from the Registry File can be taken
    over to the CA File and the search is initiated with the command
    "s L13" (here restricted to Vol. 98 only). Seventeen abstracts are
    found.

17. For the sake of comparison, a search using the term "DOS" is car-
    ried out in the same volume. The system responds with 5 answers,
    assigned to L15. That does not necessarily mean that these ab-
    stracts deal with the substance DOS with the Registry Number
    122-62-3. It could be an arbitary abbreviation for a subject term
    or a designation for a piece of equipment.

18. By asking the question "L14 or L15" and considering the answer it
    is clear that none of the 5 abstracts were found with the CAS Reg-
    istry Number. Thus, this set of 22 abtracts should be the basis
    for asking the question about the use of DOS as a plasticizer.

(19) —=> s (l13 or dos) (1) plasticiz? range=(v98,v98)
                    17 L13
                     5 DOS
                   477 PLASTICIZ?
    L17   5 (L13 OR DOS) (L) PLASTICIZ?

(20) —=> s l17 and p/dt

    L18   2 L17 AND P/DT

(21) —=> s l17 not l18
    L19   3 L17 NOT L18

(22) —=> d 1-3

    ANSWER 1

    AN   CA98(26):216464a
    TI   ...

    ANSWER 2

    AN   CA98(24):199146d
    TI   ...

(23) —=> d l18 1-2

    ANSWER 1

    AN   CA98(26):218239e
    TI   ...

    ANSWER 2

    AN   CA98(20):161778y
    TI   ...

Continuation of Fig. 92

19. The Registry Number and the term DOS are linked to the term plast-
    icizer by the proximity operator (L). As each letter of a whole
    word is compared during a search and the word plasticizer may
    occur in the plural or as an adjective in the text modifications,
    it is better to truncate the word for a search, in this case
    "plasticiz", and indicate by means of a question mark that several
    letters could follow, without specifying which letters or how
    many. Five abstracts are found.

20. The patents should be selected from answer set L17. The document
    type (dt) is entered as a patent (p). Two answers deal with pa-
    tents.

21. The remaining abstracts are recorded under L19.

22. The answers from L19 are displayed by entering the command
    "d 1-3". The same answers were found in the manual search (cf.
    Fig. 30, p. 44).

23. Both of the answers from L18 should be displayed. The manual
    search revealed only one patent abstract i.e. No. 161778.

```
①  -=>file reg
    FILE 'REGISTRY' ENTERED AT 07:41:22 ON 26 OCT 84
    COPYRIGHT 1984 BY THE AMERICAN CHEMICAL SOCIETY
②  -=>structure
③ -ENTER NAME OF STRUCTURE TO BE RECALLED (NONE):

④ —ENTER (DIS), GRA, NOD, BON OR ?:set bon se,
                                   gra r65,8 c2,r6,11 12,11 c1,11 c1,
                                   nod 9 10 n,18 19 o,
                                   bon r 1 2 rn,12 13 rn,8-10 11-18 11-19 cde,

                                   gra r6,22 c2,26 c1,26 c1,r6,27 35,
                                   nod 27 n,28 29 o,
                                   bon r 20 21 rn,26-28 26-29 cde,

                                   del 33-34,34-35,34,
                                   gra 7 35,7 33,

                                   hco 30 31 e2,32 33 e3,

                                   mov .....
                                   dis
```

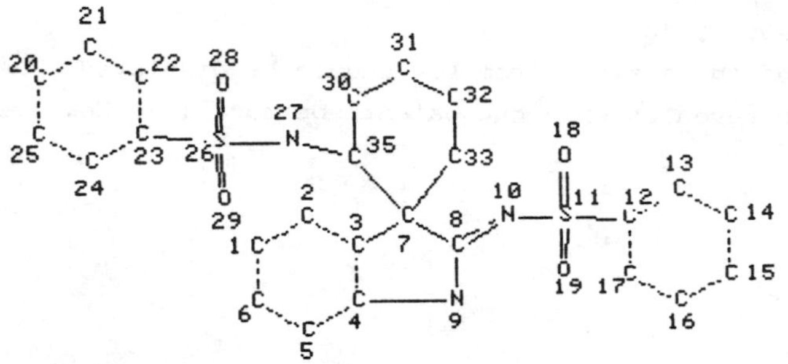

```
⑤ -ENTER (DIS), GRA, NOD, BON OR ?:end
⑥ —L2   STRUCTURE CREATED
```

(continued overleaf)

Fig. 93: Online search in the Registry File

9.3 Sample search: Have there been any publications about the follow-
                   ing substance or its derivatives? (cf. 4.3, p. 113)

        To illustrate: the Registry File

Explanation of Fig. 93:
1. Following the usual login procedure the Registry File is entered.
2. The "structure" command signifies that a structure formula will
   be entered.
3. The system responds with a prompt asking whether the structure
   has been previously recorded and should now be recalled. The
   entry of a period after the colon indicates that a new structure
   will follow (default option).
4. The system asks for the rings, nodes and bonds to be specified.
   The description of the structure is entered as text commands,
   the structure is displayed graphically (type 2 terminal). The
   commands will not be discussed here in detail (cf. chap. 8.2.1,
   p. 150). From the beginning the system numbers all the atoms so
   that each change and addition is precisely determined. The "mov"
   command can be used to alter the position of parts of the structure to give a better view of them on the screen. The structure
   diagram is displayed following the text input by using the "dis"
   command. In contrast to the manual search, no time range should
   be specified. In principle, the system assumes that every possible position can be substituted. If no substituent is desired an
   H must always be inserted.
5. A prompt automatically follows each graphically displayed structure to ask if further additions will follow. The "end" command
   signals that the structure is complete.
6. The structure is stored under L2.

⑦——=>sea l2 sss ful
　　SEARCH INITIATED (7:44:32)

⑧——:sta

　　SEARCH EXECUTING
　　　　SEARCHED   SEARCH TIME   ANSWERS   PROJECTED ANSWERS
　　　　34.840%   00.01.45   0   0 TO   0

　　:sta
⑨——FULL FILE SEARCH COMPLETE
　　　　SEARCHED   SEARCH TIME   ANSWERS
　　　　100.000%   00.04.44   2

　　:end
⑨——FULL FILE SEARCH COMPLETE
　　L3   2 SEA SSS FUL L6

⑩——=>d 1-2 sub can

⑪
⑫——RN   59238-82-3   ANS 1
　　 IN   Benzenesulfonamide,
　　 4-chloro-N-[2-[[(4-chlorophenyl)sulfonyl]amino]-1'-methylspiro[cycloh
　　 exane-1,3'-[3H]indol]-2'(1'H)-ylidene]- (9CI)
⑬
⑭——SY   Spiro[cyclohexane-1,3'-[3H]indole], benzenesulfonamide deriv. (9CI)
　　 MF   C26 H25 Cl2 N3 O4 S2

⑮——1 REFERENCES IN FILE CA (1967 TO DATE)
⑯——1   CA84(23):164559z

⑰——RN   52850-92-7   ANS 2
　　 IN   Benzenesulfonamide,
　　 N-[1',2'-dihydro-1'-methyl-2'-[[(4-methylphenyl)sulfonyl]imino]spiro[
　　 cyclohexane-1,3'-[3H]indol]-2-yl]-4-methyl- (9CI)
　　 SY   Spiro[cyclohexane-1,3'-[3H]indole], benzenesulfonamide deriv. (9CI)
　　 MF   C28 H31 N3 O4 S2

　　1 REFERENCES IN FILE CA (1967 TO DATE)
　　1   CA81(5):25490v

Continuation of Fig. 93

7. The search for the structure is initiated by the "sea" command and in this case as a substructure search (sss), as it is a substance in which some positions remain unspecified. The search should be carried out in the entire file (ful). These greatly abbreviated commands are part of the "expert version". Inexperienced searchers will probably prefer to use the longer terms, which are more easily memorized, although they take up more time.

8. While the system compares the specified structure with the 8.4 million substances in the Registry File – this can take up to five minutes –, it is possible to view (with the command sta (= status) how many percent of the file is searched in what period of time, how many answers have already been found and how many answers are to be expected based on the number already located.

9. The search is complete, the two answers are stored under L3.

10. The "sub can" command retrieves all information describing the substance with the abstract numbers.

11. RN = CAS Registry Number

12. IN = Index Name: systematic CA Index Name. The addition of 9CI denotes that this name was valid from the ninth collective period onwards.

13. SY = synonyms

14. MF = molecular formula followed by the structure diagram

15. Thereafter follows a note indicating that one reference to the substance is recorded in the CA File from 1967 till the present.

16. The CA volume number, issue number and abstract number are given.

17. The second answer is then printed.

These abstracts were also found by the manual search in the printed version of Chemical Abstracts, but the structure diagram was not so easily and rapidly obtained.

10 Final Remarks

This book illustrates the diverse ways of using the databases of the Chemical Abstract Service - both in the printed and the computer-readable version. Whether it is preferable to use the online service or execute a search manually can only be decided in each individual case, as the examples have shown. If the subject of a search is a precisely defined substance, for which the CA systematic name is known or can be derived without difficulty, or if a concept is sought which can be exactly specified with a term from the controlled vocabulary of Chemical Abstracts, then a search in the printed version of Chemical Abstracts is just as effective and often just as rapid as a computer-assisted search. And a manual search is always less expensive. If patent information is required and related patents are sought, the printed Patent Index with its cross-references and its compilation of patent families offers a unique source of information which no online service can rival.

However, when the search deals with a complex subject described by numerous terms and/or limitations, or when substructures or structures, for which the systematic nomenclature is unknown, are sought then a search in the printed version can be extremely time-consuming and the results are often very unsatifactory. In this case CAS ONLINE offers fundamentally new search possibilities and permits a much more selective formulation of the query. Today, for the first time, it is possible to carry out a search using the language of the chemist i.e. with structural formulae. Thus, the dream of a chemist has come true in part: by pressing a key he can obtain structure diagrams and literature references. However, the quality of the results depends on which key he presses i.e. what knowledge the searcher possesses about the stored data and how thoroughly he has prepared his search strategy before he begins his search.

A further advantage of a computer-assisted literature search must be emphasized: as a result of the "protocol" which is continuously printed out during an online search, input questions, the combination of search terms as well as the results can be easily reviewed and reproduced, while search terms are seldom noted after a manual search. Consequently a complete repetition of the search must be carried out in the printed services if its steps are to be examined or varied. Moreover, an online search can be subsequently processed, as the results and interim results can be stored and are always available as a starting-point for a further search.

One point about an online search should never be overlooked: that the success of a literature search not only depends on the ability and knowledge of the searcher but also on the quality of the stored information. A database is, at least in its initial stages, compiled by people, all of whom are subject to human error, so that mistakes in the storage and indexing of the information cannot be excluded. Such errors are of much greater consequence in online than in manual searches, as they can quickly lead to a dead end. Thus, there is an increasingly important demand for correct and reliable information. This demand is not only addressed to the producers of databases, e.g. the Chemical Abstracts Service, but also to authors of the primary publications who can help to prevent errors by clearly and unambiguously emphasizing the subject they have researched and precisely describing the substances which have been newly synthesized. Nowadays it is not sufficient to describe known substances with a structure formula or a substance name, these should also be supplemented by the CAS Registry Number to ensure that the substance is correctly cited later. In this way the author provides not only the basis for the correct indexing of his paper, but also enables the reader of his publication to carry out a rapid retrospective literature search.

11 Index

This index is an alphabetical list of all the keywords from the preceding chapters with references to the corresponding page numbers. For terms, which are the main subject of a whole section or several consecutive pages, the initial page number is followed by "ff"; terms, which are illustrated in detail with the help of an example, are supplemented by (E); cross-references are indicated by "s".